8.14.79

From Cell to Clone

also by Margery Facklam

Frozen Snakes and Dinosaur Bones
Exploring a Natural History Museum

Wild Animals, Gentle Women

The Story of Genetic Engineering

HBJ

From Cell

to

Clone

by Margery and Howard Facklam

Illustrated with diagrams by Paul Facklam and with photographs

Harcourt Brace Jovanovich, New York and London

Requests for permission to make copies of any part
of the work should be mailed to:
Permissions, Harcourt Brace Jovanovich, Inc.,
757 Third Avenue, New York, N.Y. 10017

The author wishes to thank Maxine Kumin for permission
to reprint the poem "The Microscope" by Maxine Kumin.
Copyright © 1963, by The Atlantic Monthly Company, Boston,
Massachusetts; and also Harper & Row, Publishers, Inc.,
for permission to reprint a quotation from *Brave New World*
by Aldous Huxley, published by Harper & Row.

Printed in the United States of America

Library of Congress Cataloging in Publication Data

Facklam, Margery.
    From cell to clone.

    Bibliography: p.
    Includes index.
    SUMMARY: Discusses genetic engineering, particularly
the history and techniques of cloning and including
material on recombinant DNA research and test-tube babies.
    1. Genetic engineering—History.   2.   Cloning—
History.   [1.   Genetic engineering.   2.   Cloning]
I.   Facklam, Howard, joint author.   II.   Facklam, Paul.
III.   Title.
QH442.F32   575.1   79–87515
ISBN 0–15–230262–X

First edition

B C D E

This book is dedicated to the
children who share our genes
and those who may help pass
them along . . . Tom and Nancy,
Dave and Susan, John and Michelle,
Paul and Terry, and Peggy Facklam

Contents

Authors' Note

Biology is an enormous subject. It covers all of life. This book tells of only one small portion, the history of the discoveries that led to the understanding of heredity, that unlocked the blueprint of life, and the way in which those discoveries are working for us now.

Many people helped us find information and photographs, but we especially wish to thank a few of the people who were generous with their time: Dr. Rosemary Elliott, Roswell Park Memorial Institute, who criticized the manuscript; Dr. Robin Bannerman, Children's Hospital, Buffalo, New York, who talked to us about genetic counseling; Donald Tartock, Director of Research at Grand Island Biological Supply, who showed us the techniques of tissue culture and plant cloning; Dr. Thomas Facklam, Battelle Institute in Columbus, Ohio, who answered his parents' questions patiently. Special thanks go to Paul Facklam, whose illustrations add so much to the book, and to Barbara Lucas and her staff at Harcourt Brace Jovanovich for ideas, encouragement, and knowing how to put a book together so well.

Margery and Howard Facklam

Snyder, New York, 1979

From Cell to Clone

1 *Recipe for Mice*

Robert Wayne slumped in the swivel chair behind his cluttered desk. He stared at the information scanner to his right but he did not listen to the too-cheery computer voice reporting the day's weather, the shuttle schedule to the space colonies, and news of another strike on the garbage convoys to the moon. He tapped nervously on the desk.

Although he had been waiting for the call, he was startled by the soft buzz of the phone. His doctor's face appeared on the screen and Mr. Wayne listened intently as the doctor read the medical report.

"You're certain, doctor? No mistake?" asked Mr. Wayne.

The doctor nodded and his voice was slower, more serious, as he said, "Absolutely certain. You will need your clone for the transplant. Shall we alert the Institute or will you?"

For several seconds Mr. Wayne did not answer. "Mr. Wayne?" the doctor prompted.

"Uh, no—I'll take care of it. Thank you." Mr. Wayne switched off the phone screen.

He did not dread the surgery so much as he dreaded the clone alert. For the first time in his life, Mr. Wayne thought seriously about his clone. It was against the law to communicate with him, but suddenly he desperately wanted to meet and talk with him—this stranger who was an exact physical copy of himself.

Families who could afford it were allowed to order Clone #1 to be started immediately after the birth of a child. So Mr. Wayne's clone was only a few weeks younger than he. A person's first clone was required to be a resident of the health farm run by the National Institute of Cloned Humans. There the clones were raised with great care and under the best medical control. These clones had no contact with anyone except the Institute staff. Although no one said so in public, people called these farms the spare parts farms. It was comforting to know that a clone was always available for blood transfusions, as a stand-in for possible allergic reactions to new medication, or for transplants, but it was a subject seldom discussed. It was frankly easier not to think about it at all.

Now, however, Mr. Wayne wondered how his clone felt about his alert. This was only a kidney transplant. It would not take the clone's life, but what if it had been a heart transplant? How were the clones trained to accept that? Well, that was not his responsibility.

For those who could afford a second, Clone #2 was a personal copy raised in the intellectual community controlled by the best universities. Mr. Wayne often wished he had a Clone #2, one who could help him in his business or with occasional knotty personal problems. These were the clones that proved the old adage that two heads are better than one.

Mr. Wayne knew a few fortunate people who also had the ultimate luxury, Clone #3, a personable, socially acceptable double to appear for its single parent at cocktail parties or attend piano recitals given by the children of friends.

Science fiction? Of course; at least for now.

When your grandfather was a child, however, heart transplants and moon walks were science fiction. And scientists do know how to clone. It is done all the time in laboratories with plants and lower forms of animal life. Although the cloning of a man is still in a science-fiction category, it might not be for long. They know *how* to do it, and with better microsurgical techniques and a few more biological clues, they will be able to do it.

Many people are frightened at the prospect of cloning because they see it as the science-fiction story of Mr. Wayne and his duplicates. But any discovery can be used for good or evil. Fire can destroy or cook. Atomic energy can destroy or can keep factories running. Drugs can destroy a body and a mind or ease the pain of critically ill people and help stabilize mental disorders. Discoveries in biology that make cloning possible can make life better for humans in many ways.

Every age has its science fiction, and probably the fears that go with it. In the 1770s when the United States of America was being pulled together out of struggling colonies, many people in the community, hearing about new inventions and discoveries, would shake their heads and mutter about the evils they would bring. Had they known the phrase, they would have called them science fiction.

At the same time there was a group of men in England that the newspapers nicknamed the "Lunatics." They met once a month on a night of the full moon for the sensible reason that they could ride home on horseback more easily by moonlight. The real name of the group was the Lunar Society of Birmingham, and its members met to discuss religion, politics, poetry, business, and science. They were men of mixed backgrounds, mixed interests, and not one had a job that could be described as that of a full-time scientist.

It was not a time of great intellectual freedom. Schools were for the privileged class. The members of this "invisible college" were for the most part wealthy men. Science was a rich man's hobby, the avocation of men with other means of support. Some were chemists or doctors who had laboratories. They were men who had the kind of curiosity that is as much a part of a scientist as is the trained mind. The great nineteenth-century French chemist Louis Pasteur said, "In the field of observation, chance favors the prepared mind." He was talking about "accidental discoveries." They are accidental only in that the discoverer who tripped over them had a mind that allowed him to put together the right clues.

The Scotsman James Watt, inventor of the condensing steam engine, was a Lunatic, as was the grandfather of the great evolutionist Charles Darwin and himself an evolutionist. William Herschel, bandmaster by profession but astronomer by interest, discussed the many discoveries he had made with the assistance of his sister Caroline. Many years after her death she was recognized as a brilliant astronomer in her own right. Joseph Priestley, who isolated the gas oxygen from the air, corresponded with Benjamin Franklin in the American colonies and told the other members of the society about Franklin's experiment with the kite.

But few of these Lunatics or other educated men of the time were investigating biology as a laboratory science. Biology was classifying, collecting, studying relationships of animals rather than what made them work.

Microscopes were known and used. The great Italian astronomer Galileo Galilei had built microscopes, along with telescopes, more than a century earlier, but they were crude instruments. There was no concentrated effort to find the key to life. It is hard to find something if you have no idea what you are looking for. Finding a needle in a haystack is impossible if you don't know what a needle is.

One theory was like the Chinese box puzzle in which there are boxes inside of boxes inside of boxes. The teachers of this theory believed that Eve had produced an egg which contained miniatures of all the people who would ever be born. An eighteenth-century mathematician predicted that this would be 27 million people, close to the population of California today.

Another theory described the "homunculus" or "little man that grew inside the sperm." Perhaps the artist who drew the homunculus imagined that the colors and shadings he saw through a crude microscope were in the shape of a tiny human. These believers were called the spermists, and they thought that Adam had carried the seeds that would create all mankind forever.

A third group believed in epigenesis, which meant that the blood and other matter in the mother's womb was "organized" into a baby by contact with the sperm.

The authority on most of these matters was Aristotle, a Greek philosopher who lived between the years 384 B.C. and 322 B.C. With little variation, the life science taught in schools for centuries came from Aristotle. Isaac Asimov, a scientist and science writer of today, said that Aristotle's ideas came to be regarded as almost divine, so that if Aristotle said it was so, it was *so*.

Aristotle tackled all subjects—politics, ethics, mathematics— but he seemed especially prolific in the field of biology. He wrote 150 volumes on plants and animals. He classified 500 animals,

An alchemist searches for the substance that will create human life, the homunculus or miniature man in the crucible. (The Bettmann Archive)

sometimes quite against the ideas of his time. For example, he watched the dolphin feed its young with milk and correctly classified it as a mammal, although it was centuries before anyone else agreed.

Along with his good guesses, Aristotle made some monumental errors, such as the idea that the brain was merely a cooling device for the blood and the center of life, mind, and all emotion was the heart. He could not believe what he could not see. He opposed the theory of another Greek teacher, Democritus, who said that all things were made up of small units called atoms. Aristotle could not see an atom and he couldn't believe in them.

Of all Aristotle's theories, the one most difficult for science to shake was that of spontaneous generation. It persisted in one form or another for almost 2,000 years.

Spontaneous generation meant that life could spring from non-living material. In his book *Historia Animalium*, Aristotle wrote that "every dry body which becomes moist and every humid body which dries up breeds life."

Some fish laid eggs that could be seen, but no one knew where eels came from. Aristotle said eels grew from "slime and ooze at the bottom of rivers and oceans." He taught that some insects are born on the dew on leaves or from hair, flesh, or excrement of animals.

There was no reason for people not to believe in spontaneous generation. They could see skinny little horse hair worms wriggling in pools and thought they must have come from hairs from a horse's tail that had fallen into the water. They saw the goose-shaped barnacles on the rocks along the ocean shore and had every reason to believe they were the young of the barnacle goose that swam along the same shore. They were the same color and similar in shape, and no one had seen the eggs of the barnacle goose anywhere. They saw flies emerge from rotting meat and decaying flesh, and it followed that rotting meat gave birth to flies.

If anyone doubted Aristotle's theory, there is no record of it for hundreds of years. Toward the end of the 1500s, a physician in Brussels, Jan Baptista van Helmont, believed so strongly in spontaneous generation that he wrote, "The emanations arising from the bottom of marshes brings forth frogs, snails, leeches, herbs, and a good many other things."

He even offered a recipe for mice: Take one dirty shirt and a

People thought the goose barnacle grew into the barnacle goose.

few grains of corn. Place them in an old pot. At the end of twenty-one days a lively crop of mice will be produced.

Another common "recipe" advised taking a young bull, killing him with a knock on the head, and burying him standing with only his horns sticking out of the ground. Leave him for a month, then saw off his horns, and out will fly a swarm of bees.

The Church added its blessing to the theory when Saint Augustine wrote that spontaneous generation was a means by which God demonstrated his omnipotence, his power over all, by interfering with the usual orderly sequence of events, by stepping in to create something out of nothing.

As time went on, however, some people were skeptical enough to look for new answers. Late in the 1600s, an Italian physician, Francesco Redi, read a small book that had been published by the English physician William Harvey in 1628. Harvey described how blood circulates, a discovery he kept to himself for thirteen years for fear of reprisals from the Church. In this book, Harvey also suggested that small living things might arise from unseen eggs and seeds and not from non-living matter at all. Redi decided to test the idea with some experiments. His tests are the first recorded experiments in biology that used proper controls so there could be no doubt as to their accuracy.

Redi decided to tackle the problem of flies growing from rotting meat. He put meat in eight flasks. He left four of the flasks open. Flies could go in and out. He sealed four of the flasks so no flies could get at the rotting meat.

Of course there were maggots all over the rotting meat in the open flasks and no maggots in the sealed jars. Just to make sure that it wasn't the air that caused the reproduction of flies, he repeated the experiment. This time he covered four flasks with fine netting so that air could circulate but flies could not get in. Again four flasks were left open. He got the same results, proving that the meat was not producing flies but that the flies themselves were reproducing. It seems like an obvious conclusion now, but it was not then.

Redi's experiments should have put an end to the spontaneous generation discussions, but, just about the time that he was making them, Anton van Leeuwenhoek, a Dutchman, was looking at "wee beasties" in his extraordinary microscopes. What he saw was convincing evidence for some people that these "wee beasties" came spontaneously from nowhere, and it would be another 200 years before experiments proved that all living things are created by other living things.

How did we get from spontaneous generation and the homunculus to test-tube babies and cloning? How did we move from recipes for mice to the modern DNA experiments that actually change the basic construction of living things?

We have to go back to the basic unit of life to find out.

2 *The Relay Race*

THE MICROSCOPE

Anton Leeuwenhoek was Dutch.
He sold pincushions, cloth, and such.
The waiting townsfolk fumed and fussed
As Anton's dry goods gathered dust.

He worked, instead of tending store,
At grinding special lenses for
A microscope. Some of the things
He looked at were:

                      mosquitoes' wings,
the hairs of sheep, the legs of lice,
the skin of people, dogs, and mice;
ox eyes, spiders' spinning gear,
fishes' scales, a little smear
of his own blood,

                    and best of all,
the unknown, busy, very small
bugs that swim and bump and hop
inside a simple water drop,

Impossible! most Dutchmen said.
This Anton's crazy in the head.

We ought to ship him off to Spain.
He says he's seen a housefly's brain.
He says the water that we drink
Is full of bugs. He's mad, we think!

They called him dumkopf, which means dope.
That's how we got the microscope.

Maxine Kumin

Every living thing, porcupine, porpoise, or pineapple, is made up of cells. And *everything* a living thing does is done by the cells that make it up. That is the rule; no exceptions.

Without cells we cannot breathe, read a book, pet a dog, ride a skateboard, or eat popcorn. Without cells there would be no popcorn.

There are nerve cells, muscle cells, bone cells, red blood cells, skin cells, scale cells on a snake, some cells as large as the ostrich egg, but most of them so tiny that they can be seen only with a microscope. While each cell works separately, using energy, reproducing, getting rid of wastes, together they allow plants and animals to function, to live. There are 60,000 billion cells in a human being, all working together, breathing, reproducing, using energy, getting rid of wastes.

No wonder the processes of life have always been surrounded by myth, mystery, and miracles.

Compared to the length of time man has been on earth, several million years, we have known about cells only for a split second. No one ever heard of a cell until 1665, when a twenty-nine-year-old Englishman, Robert Hooke, published a small book dedicated to King Charles II with the inscription, "I do most humbly lay this small present at your Majesties' Royal feet." It was worthy of a royal presentation.

The book was called *Microphagia, or Some Physiological Descriptions of Minute Bodies Made by Magnifying Glasses with Observations and Inquiries Thereupon.* It was published at a time when most people had other things on their minds. The Great Plague was killing thousands of people, sweeping unchecked across England and the continent. A great fire destroyed most of London. In spite of the turmoil, Hooke's little book caused quite a stir among educated people, the kind of men who had formed the Royal Society of London and the Lunar Society.

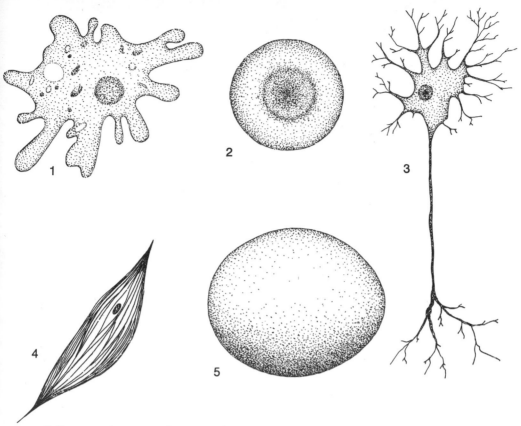

Cells come in many shapes and sizes.

1. Amoeba, a one-celled animal
2. A red blood cell
3. A nerve cell
4. A muscle cell
5. The largest cell, an ostrich egg

Descriptions of men in history are handed down from biographer to biographer and Hooke has been labeled as an antisocial, nasty, quarrelsome sort of person. It is said that he drove Sir Isaac Newton to a nervous breakdown. We can never really know, nor does it really matter except that this description might explain why Hooke moved from one thing to another, why he never went further with his cell discovery.

Hooke was orphaned when he was eight years old and in the custom of the time he was sent out as an apprentice, to work and learn a trade. Hooke's teacher-employer was an artist, from whom he must have learned much, because the illustrations he made for *Microphagia* are still among the best ever done of microscopic life.

Hooke inherited just enough money to allow him to enter Oxford University, and while he was there he was hired as an assistant to a wealthy young man, Robert Boyle, the fourteenth child of the Earl of Cork. It was lucky for both men. Hooke liked to tinker, to work with anything mechanical, and it was he who designed and built the air pump later described in Boyle's first book. Many scientists think that Hooke had an important part in developing Boyle's Law, which has to do with the volume and pressure of gas in relation to temperature.

Because of his work at Oxford, Hooke was hired by the newly formed Royal Society as its Curator of Experiments; he was its only paid employee. Part of his job was to present "three or four considerable experiments" at weekly meetings.

Hooke had been grinding lenses and he put together a compound microscope, one using two lenses, a crude piece of equipment by today's standards, but quite remarkable at the time. It was lighted with a candle reflected in a lens. He took one of his microscopes to a Royal Society meeting and amazed the members with his observations.

With a sharp razor he had sliced off the thinnest section of cork he could manage. Under the microscope the cork appeared to be built of a series of tiny cubicles. "I could exceedingly plainly perceive it all to be perforated and porous, much like a Honeycomb," he wrote. The sections looked like the tiny cubicles used by monks in monasteries, rooms called cells, so Hooke called them cells. He looked at "carrets, daucus, Bur-docks, teasel, fearn, and several kinds of reeds." And in all of them he found "an infinite company of small Boxes or Bladders of Air."

But Hooke went no further with his investigations. Some say it was because he was rebuilding projects destroyed in the London fire, others say he lost interest and moved on to other projects. However, he had named the basic structure of life, the importance of which he would never know.

This was about the same time that Anton van Leeuwenhoek was also working with microscopes. He was not a trained scientist. He could read no Latin, the language of scientists, so he did not know of Hooke's discovery. Some historians say that Leeuwenhoek's lack of training allowed him to trust his own eyes, his own

Robert Hooke used a
compound microscope
similar to this when
he found the cells
in the cork.

thoughts, his own judgment, because he was cut off from all the "learned nonsense" of his time.

Like Hooke, Leeuwenhoek had served as an apprentice. He was sixteen when his father died and he went to work in a draper's shop in Amsterdam, a shop that sold fabrics. Perhaps he became fascinated with lenses as he examined the weave and threads of the fabrics with a magnifying glass, but he became extremely skillful at making lenses and at working with the precious metals in which he mounted the lenses.

There is little record of what he did for almost twenty years. We know he married and moved to the city of Delft, where he opened his own draper's shop. He continued work on his absorbing hobby.

Hooke had used two lenses, making a compound microscope, but the lenses were not of good quality, which limited what he could see. Leeuwenhoek made simple, single-lens instruments, but they were of such exquisite craftsmanship that they allowed him to see into a new world. He watched the "wretched beasties" he saw swimming, dividing, engulfing food, and he could hardly believe the life in a drop of water. His microscopes magnified up to 200 times, and frequently he mounted an object permanently to the instrument, making a new microscope when he wanted to see another kind of "wee beastie."

Today Leeuwenhoek would be called an oddball, a character, a true individualist. Perhaps people called him such things then, too. But thank goodness for such individuals. He did not care what the community thought. He took a "bit of white matter" from his teeth and found some "tiny animalcules, very prettily a-moving." He looked at insect wings, animal hairs, parasites on fleas. In fact, his observations became so well known that Jonathan Swift, the author of *Gulliver's Travels*, wrote about his work:

> "So naturalists observe, a flea
> Has smaller fleas that on him prey;
> And these have smaller still to bite 'em;
> And so proceed ad infinitum."

Leeuwenhoek correctly identified human sperm but he was afraid to say too much about it for fear of being thought obscene.

It wasn't until Leeuwenhoek was forty-one years old that he became known to other scientists. A physician friend of his, Regnier de Graaf, sent some of Leeuwenhoek's papers to the Royal Society in London. The members were astounded and amazed. They asked their Curator of Experiments, Robert Hooke, to verify Leeuwenhoek's findings. After a false start or two, Hooke also found the "animalcules" reported by the Dutch draper.

Leeuwenhoek was immensely pleased to have his work accepted by such a prestigious group, especially since he had no education himself. During the next fifty years, he sent 375 long rambling letters to the society, telling of his observations as well as the state of his health, the weather, and gossip from the city of Delft.

In 1680, he was made a Fellow of the Royal Society, and in gratitude for this honor he sent the society twenty-six of his microscopes. But he would never tell how he made them. No one has been able to figure out how he got such clarity in his lenses with the equipment available to him, and his secret died with him. Some experts think that, instead of grinding the perfect little lenses for his

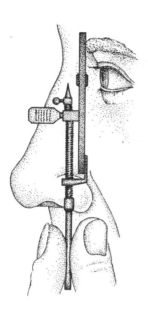

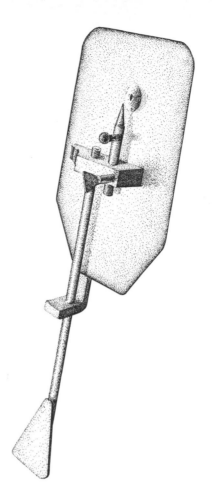

Leeuwenhoek's microscope
was held up to the eye to
see an object that could
be permanently mounted.

Leeuwenhoek's microscope

hand-held microscopes, Leeuwenhoek made them from a drop of molten glass. Although his lenses were crude compared to those today, they were exceptional then, and it is unfortunate that only eight of them still exist.

Hooke coined the word "cell" and Leeuwenhoek found living protozoa and simple algae, but no one put the observations together. The connection was not made to show that cells are living things, and hundreds of years passed before anything more was discovered about the cell.

A German naturalist, Lorenz Oken, offered a cell theory in 1805. "All organic beings originate from and consist of vesicles or cells." But if his idea caused any stir in the scientific world it died quickly.

A quarter of a century later, a botanist in Scotland came up with some more information about the cell. Robert Brown had been trained as a doctor but he was more interested in botany. He obtained a position on a ship going to the almost unknown continent of Australia, and he brought back 4,000 species of plants. He classified his collection with great care, examining many specimens under the microscope. He found what he described as an "opake spot" in the cells of orchids and, checking with other plants, found these spots in all the cells. He named the spot the nucleus, which, in Latin, means "little nut."

Although we know now that the nucleus is the "main office" of the cell, Brown had no idea how important it was. This nucleus

A cell, with the nucleus clearly defined, magnified 8,000 times with an electron microscope. (State University of Buffalo at New York)

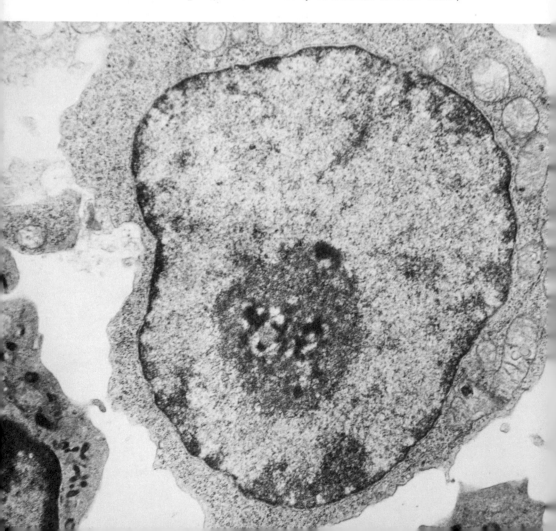

A section of the skin of an onion showing a fine network of elongated cells closely cemented together. (Dr. Lewis R. Wolberg, *Zooming In*, HBJ, 1974.)

office sends out instructions to the rest of the cell, telling it what products should be made and how much of them. In this office are the complete blueprints for the cell factory so that a new and identical factory can be built from those plans.

Charles Darwin consulted Brown before he went on his famous voyage on the *Beagle* in 1831, but he found Brown to be a "scientific miser." Brown kept all his information to himself. He announced the discovery of the nucleus and that was that. Darwin wrote of him, "His knowledge was extraordinarily great, and much died with him, owing to his excessive fear of ever making a mistake."

The sharing of knowledge is the lifeblood of scientific investigation, which is very much like a great relay race. It is a race run not on a clear, straight course but through a maze with many wrong turns, many blind alleys. Each worker is like a runner picking up the baton of the one before him, carrying it as far as he can. Sometimes the baton is dropped and no one picks it up for a long time, and sometimes it is passed from hand to hand rapidly with fact quickly added to fact. More and more science has become a team effort with many people attacking problems from different angles with different techniques.

Once in a while there are some sideline activities that make progress a little faster.

Early in the 1800s, one of the problems in cell study was cutting sections of plants or animals to look at under a microscope. This required a sharp razor, like those used in barber shops, and it was necessary to cut the thinnest, most uniform slice possible. It wasn't always successful. Sometimes a cell structure would be visible, but in another section, which might be too thick, it would not be seen at all.

In the 1830s, as a very useful sideline activity, Jan Purkinje, a Czechoslovakian biologist, invented a piece of equipment called the microtome, which solved this problem. It was a simple machine much like a bologna slicer at a meat market, except that it was more accurate, more delicate, and much smaller. A piece of tissue to be studied is mounted in a piece of paraffin which can then be sliced into ultrathin slices guaranteed to be the same every time.

Today, instead of using paraffin, it is common to quick-freeze the tissue with liquid nitrogen. For use with the electron microscope, tissue is put into plastic and cut with a diamond blade in an ultramicrotome. These sections are so superfine that the operator must watch through a binocular microscope as he uses the ultramicrotome.

The next to pick up the baton in the scientific relay were two nineteenth-century German biologists, Dr. Matthias Jacob Schleiden and Dr. Theodor Schwann. They met at a dinner party and began a conversation that finally led to the great major concept of biology, the theory that all living things are made up of units called cells.

Dr. Schleiden, who had been a lawyer before he became a botanist, was eloquently describing to his dinner companion his theory that all plants are made up entirely of cells and that plant growth is the formation of cells from cells.

As Dr. Schleiden talked, Dr. Schwann got more and more excited because he had been studying animal cells. The problem seemed to be that neither he nor other anatomists could find basic cells in animal tissue. There were too many kinds of cells, too many shapes and sizes to suggest any basic sameness. But as Dr. Schwann listened to his dinner companion, some pieces of the puzzle began to fall into place.

It may not have been a memorable dinner for the other guests, but it was for the two scientists. They could hardly wait to begin a thorough investigation of animal cells. They knew that it would take a lot of work to convince the scientific world that the diversity of structure in plants and animals had its basis in cells. It would take real proof to convince people that even such dead tissue as hoofs, nails, and hair grew from cells.

It took them a year to finish their study. In 1839, Schleiden and Schwann published a book that presented the cell theory. "There is one universal principle of development for the elementary parts of organisms however different," they wrote, "and this principle is the formation of cells."

We take the cell theory so much for granted, it seems so simple and obvious, that it is difficult to remember that it is one of the great concepts of science. It was as important to biology as the discovery of atoms was to physics.

On the hundredth anniversary of the publication of the cell theory, the American Association for the Advancement of Science had a huge celebration to honor Schleiden and Schwann. The main speaker astounded the audience, however, not with praise for the two biologists, but with words of scorn. He declared that the credit for the theory belonged not to Schleiden and Schwann but to Hooke and Brown and all biologists before them. He said that the German biologists had only summarized what others had learned.

The speaker was right in that regard, although he could reasonably have given credit to the winning team in that particular relay. No discovery is ever made in a vacuum, apart from all the knowledge that has gone before it. No scientific discovery stands alone.

One great insight, one great theory or discovery, may come from the mind of a single person, but that person had to be in the right place at the right time. That person had to have the prepared mind. He picked up the baton in the great race.

In many ways, Aristotle is still not out of date. He wrote, "Each adds a little to our knowledge of Nature, and from all the facts assembled arises grandeur."

So it was with the cell, and we have not even begun to unlock all its secrets.

3 *Probability in a Pea Patch*

As people were beginning to hear about Schleiden's and Schwann's cell theory, another branch of science was growing in a pea patch in Austria. It was the science that would explain why everyone in a family had brown eyes or why one child in a family has dark curly hair and two others have straight blond hair. It was the science that also would explain why some people are born with diseases or defects.

Gregor Mendel was a monk whose profession was teaching. His hobby was puttering in his garden. He was born in 1822 to a poor peasant family and in the local school he learned beekeeping and horticulture. Until he entered the monastery he helped his father tend the gardens that fed the family. The order he belonged to supplied teachers to the local schools, but Mendel did not pass the examinations for a teaching certificate. Three times he failed them, doing very poorly on the biology questions because he had no formal training. The abbot of the monastery recognized some special talents in the young monk, however, and sent him to the University of Vienna in 1851.

When Mendel finished college he returned to the monastery and became an inspired teacher of mathematics and science at the

Gregor Mendel. (The Bettmann Archive)

Modern School in the city of Brünn. He truly enjoyed teaching, but he seemed to find special joy in tending the monastery gardens. Like all good scientists before him, and all to come, Mendel was a keen observer, and he thought about what he saw. He was insatiably curious.

He noticed, among other things, that whenever he planted seeds from tall plants, he got tall plants. Seeds from short plants produced short plants. But sometimes there were mixed patches of plants, too, some tall and some short. He noticed patterns in other traits among his patch of sweet peas, too, traits for colors or position of the flowers or smoothness of seeds.

In 1857 Mendel decided to begin the long study that would be necessary to explain what he saw happening. He knew it would be an enormous job because in the beginning of one of his reports he wrote, "It indeed required some courage to undertake such far-reaching labors."

He planned the experiment with great care, setting aside a plot that measured 6 meters by 30 meters in which he would raise the sweet peas.

The first step was to make sure the seeds he used were "pure" —that is that these seeds would produce only one kind of plant. In order to do this he carefully wrapped each plant with bits of calico so that no pollen would escape, so that no plant would be accidentally fertilized by pollen on the legs of a passing bee. When that first crop of peas produced seeds, he collected them and stored them in jars to wait for the spring planting time.

The following spring he planted all the seeds from tall plants in marked rows. He planted all the seeds from short plants in another section of the garden. Again, he waited and weeded and protected his plants. As he expected, the seeds from tall plants produced more tall plants; they were "pure." The same was true for the short plants. He collected the seeds, and waited for the next step of the experiment in the spring.

That first generation of plants had been what Mendel called purebreds. Sometimes we say they "bred true." For the next generation, Mendel decided to cross-breed the plants. That spring, when the tall plants and the short plants came up in separate sections of the garden, Mendel took pollen from tall plants and fertilized short plants. He waited for those seeds to mature. He collected them, saved them, and planted them. When the plants from that cross-pollinating came up, they were all tall. They all looked alike, but Mendel was certain that there must be a trait for shortness carried somewhere even though it was hidden. He called that group of plants hybrids.

Carefully saving the seeds from these hybrids, Mendel waited for the next spring planting time. When the plants grew from those hybrid seeds, Mendel found an interesting pattern. This time, out of 1,064 plants, he counted 787 tall plants and 277 short plants. It was three to one for the tall plants.

Gregor Mendel knew nothing about chromosomes or genes, but he reasoned that somehow the male and female carried messages and that some of these messages were more powerful than others. He called the powerful messages dominant, and the less powerful messages he called recessive. That hybrid planting of three to one had shown him that tallness in peas was dominant and shortness was recessive.

His special contribution—the thing no one had done before—was the careful counting and comparing. For seven years Mendel planted and counted, keeping records which began to tell a story that did not change.

Gregor Mendel showed that characteristics or traits do not blend into some middle ground but keep their own identity. The pairs of characteristics, some from each parent, might combine, but they sorted themselves out according to a fixed and predictable set of rules.

When Mendel experimented with other traits the rules stayed the same. He worked with wrinkled seeds and smooth seeds and he found that the smooth seeds were dominant, that they carried more powerful messages than those for wrinkled seeds. Wrinkled seeds were recessive; smooth seeds dominant.

Mendel applied the laws of mathematics and probability to the sweet peas and came up with the science of inheritance, the science we now call genetics.

In February 1865 the Brünn Society for the Study of Natural Science was holding a meeting at the Modern School where Mendel taught. He was invited to read his paper about the sweet peas. He spoke for an hour to a quiet audience, too quiet. No one asked a question. There was no discussion. No one had ever heard of applying the laws of mathematics to flowers. They could not believe that heredity was a giant game of cards that were constantly shuffled and reshuffled.

The patient monk was extremely disappointed. Imagine working seven years on a project, knowing the thrill of seeing a pattern

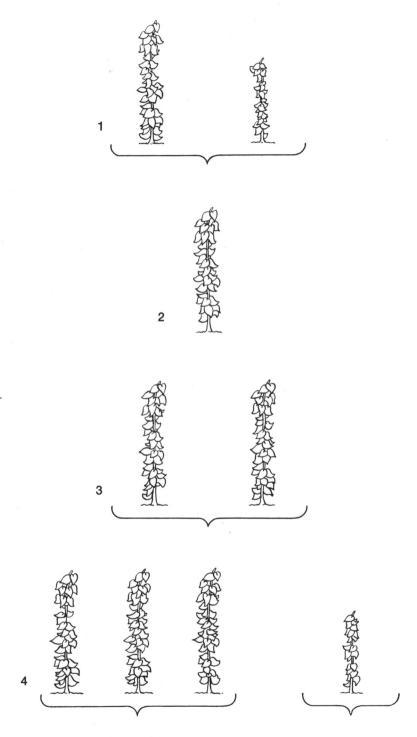

From Cell to Clone

emerge, a fact become evident, only to have it fall flat. He would probably have preferred to be openly disbelieved rather than to be almost ignored.

Mendel was humble enough to seek the advice of a botanist with more training than he, and he sent the paper to him in Munich asking him to read the study. That botanist rudely dismissed Mendel's ideas, maybe because he could not understand the mathematics and diagrams. He suggested Mendel do more work, perhaps try other plants.

Soon after, Mendel was appointed abbot of the monastery, and he was too busy to tend his pea patch as carefully as necessary for scientific study. He had also grown too fat to bend over easily to pull weeds and tie the calico bags around the seed pods. He put his paper away on a library shelf and no one heard of it again for thirty-five years.

It was one of those blind alleys. The baton was dropped while other discoveries were made, while other minds were being prepared to put Mendel's laws of inheritance to work.

One of these prepared minds was that of Hugo De Vries, another physician turned botanist. Although he studied medicine and earned an M.D., De Vries became a professor of botany at the University of Amsterdam in 1878. He was curious about new species, about the way in which a new variety of flower appeared in a field. He moved into a country house near a field of primroses and as Mendel had done, he began a long study. During twenty years he raised and kept records of more than 50,000 primrose plants and he found eight new species, eight different plants. He called these new types of plants "mutants," from the Latin word which means "to change."

Mendel's experiment

1. A tall pea plant and a short pea plant are cross pollinated.
2. Seeds from that crossing grow into tall plants called hybrids. Although they appear tall, they carry the genes for shortness, too.
3. If seeds from the cross fertilization of two hybrid tall plants are planted . . .
4. . . . they will produce a mixture in the ratio of three to one: three tall plants for every short plant, or three of the dominant characteristic for every one of the recessive characteristic.

Farmers knew all about such changes, only they called the changed plants and animals "sports." They took advantage of sports when the change was for the better. If a sheep was born with short legs which kept it from jumping over fences, they bred that sheep until they had a generation of many short-legged sheep. A farmer who found a strain of wheat with an especially good yield, or one that grew well in spite of drought or disease, planted that changed wheat seed until he had developed a whole new field of better wheat.

De Vries put practice and theory together and came up with some laws of inheritance and mutation. Then he searched the literature. Searching the literature is as much a part of scientific research as the records and the observations and experiments. The scientist has to know who has done what. De Vries found a paper on hybrid plants written by a German scientist. In that paper was a note about another paper written a generation earlier by an Austrian monk, Gregor Mendel.

De Vries found Mendel's paper, the one that had been ignored and put on a shelf. He must have been astounded to see that his theory, his work, had all been done by this monk years before. At the same time two other scientists, also unknown to De Vries, worked out the same laws of heredity.

Isaac Asimov wrote, "It is one of the most glorious chapters in scientific history that not one of the three men made any effort to claim credit for a discovery that, intellectually at least, was independently their own and which would have meant great fame." It would have been easy for them. Who else had ever heard of Gregor Mendel's sweet peas? But Hugo De Vries, as well as a German scientist, Karl Correns, a month later, and a Viennese botanist, Erich Tschermak, about three months later, announced in 1900 that they had found Mendel's theory to be right. Although each of these men thought he had found someting new, each was willing to confirm Mendel's work. From that time on the laws of inheritance have been referred to as Mendelian.

Finally, the pattern and plan of life was becoming evident. A new century had begun and it would bring with it the knowledge of the innermost workings of the cell. Just a few more steps were necessary until we would know not only how these laws of heredity worked but how to change them, control them.

4 *Back to the Microscope*

The peas and the primroses gave birth to the laws of heredity, but for many years nothing much happened to the study of the cell. In 1839, Schleiden and Schwann had announced that all living things are made of cells, but that was about it. Scientists were like bricklayers who know how many shapes and sizes of buildings can be built of bricks but who do not know of what the bricks are made.

Then in 1869, while the United States was mopping up after the Civil War, a Swiss biochemist, Friedrich Miescher, was doing graduate work. His professor suggested that he make a chemical analysis of the cell. He was having trouble breaking down all parts of the cell when he got the idea of "digesting" it with stomach enzymes.

Miescher went to a local hospital and collected bandages that had been used on infections. He used the pus from the bandages as his source of cells. When he treated them with the digestive juices, the cells broke down into their chemical parts but left a residue from the nucleus. The residue was a unique material, and Miescher called it "nuclein." His teacher would not let him publish his results for two years while he retested them himself and found the same substance in yeast cells.

The Rhine River near Miescher's home was known to fishermen as a great place to catch salmon. Miescher was often among the anglers there, but he was combining pleasure with business. He was collecting salmon sperm because it has very large nuclei, almost half the weight of the cell itself, and Miescher was able to accumulate a good supply of his newly found nuclein. He discovered during his work that nuclein was composed of carbon, oxygen, hydrogen, nitrogen, and phosphorus. He never published his work; he was always too busy. After he died in 1895, his friends published his facts about nuclein.

Jars and jars of white sticky powder, the nuclein, stood on the shelves of Miescher's laboratory for years. He had actually discovered the real key to life, but he did not know it. There it was, isolated and waiting—the heart of the heart of the cell, the "computer center" in the "nucleus office."

The microtome had solved one of the problems of cell biology, but there were others. When looking at a drop of water under a microscope it is difficult to see the transparent cells. It is necessary to dye or stain the cells in order to see them clearly.

In 1855, a seventeen-year-old boy in England had accidentally discovered something that not only started a new industry but also revealed the inner workings of the cell.

William Perkin was probably the kind of student who today would enter science fairs, because, even though he worked as a chemistry lab assistant, he was always running experiments in his lab at home, too.

At that time it was commonly and accurately said that the sun never set on the British Empire. Many of England's colonies were in the tropics and people returning from duty there had recurring bouts of malaria. Malaria was treated with quinine, also from the tropics. Perkin's employer suggested that they might try to synthesize quinine, to make it chemically. Quinine is too complex a substance to be duplicated by methods known then, but not knowing this, young Perkin went right ahead.

He started with coal-tar chemicals which were readily available. He mixed one, called aniline, with some potassium dichromate and found he had nothing but a mess of purple goo in his flask. Instead of throwing it away, he mixed it with alcohol and a beautiful purple color dissolved out.

A series of tests showed that his new purple was a wonderful permanent dye. Today people take courses to learn how to make natural dyes from roots, leaves, berries, and bark. But until the moment Perkin mixed his purple mess, natural dyes were all there were to use. Blues and purples came from the indigo plant and great industries thrived on cultivating indigo and shipping it to the weaving mills of England.

Because he was under eighteen, Perkin could not get a patent on his discovery right away, but by the time he was twenty-three, he owned and operated a large aniline dye factory. Quite unintentionally he had opened up the field of microbiology, although its development took another twenty-five years.

In 1880, Walter Flemming, a German anatomy professor, stained some cells with Perkin's aniline dye. Suddenly the "opake spot" Robert Brown had described fifty years earlier, the nuclein material Miescher had isolated, became quite clear. Flemming called the mass of colored material in the nucleus "chromatin," from the Greek word meaning color.

When Flemming stained sections of growing tissue, he saw cells in the process of dividing. He watched the chromatin bunch up into short, threadlike bodies and he called these "chromosomes," meaning colored bodies. As he studied the bunching-up process, he saw these chromosomes double in number. Next they seemed to get all tangled in a starlike structure he called the "aster," which means star in Greek. (Scientists use Greek or Latin words to name things because they will be understood universally.)

He watched the doubled chromosomes begin to pull apart. Half of them moved to one end of the cell, half to the opposite end. Because these chromosomes spread out like threads during this process, Flemming called the process "mitosis," which means thread in Greek. Half the chromosomes moved into one of the new daughter cells that formed when the cell itself pulled apart, and half went into the other new cell. They were exact duplicates. Each cell had the same amount of this chromosomal material.

When he wrote about mitosis and chromosomes in 1882, Flemming did not connect it to inheritance. Gregor Mendel's laws of heredity had not yet been rediscovered, and if Flemming suspected a connection he did not say so.

Things moved along quickly after the cell was revealed by staining. Five years later, Eduard van Beneden, a biologist in Belgium building on Flemming's work, showed that every cell in a

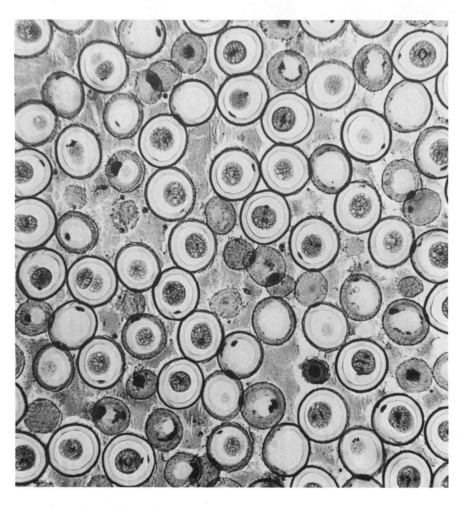

Cells seen through an electron microscope. The chromosomes in the cells are clearly visible during mitosis (cell division). (Dr. Lewis R. Wolberg, *Zooming In*, HBJ, 1974.)

body has the same number of chromosomes, with one exception. That exception is the sex cell. Either a sperm or an egg contains half of the usual number of chromosomes.

Beneden also found out that there is a characteristic number of chromosomes for a species. A human has 46, a goldfish 94, a frog 26, and a fruit fly 8. Number of chromosomes has nothing to do with size. A crayfish has 200, while the giant sequoia tree has 22. A dog has 52 and a rat has 42.

All cells, no matter whether they come from the fruit fly with its 8 chromosomes or the goldfish with its 94, work like the bricks of a house, but they are magic bricks that manufacture all other bricks. Without waiting for the architect's plans, or a foreman, or even the bricklayer, the bricks build themselves into a house. Not only that, they change to become different materials. They become the glass for the windows, water for the kitchen, or tiles for the roof. The cells—the magic bricks—seem to know what the future body will look like and how it will work. If the cells are to make a goldfish they know it, and they know how to make the fins, the scales, and the gills. More than that, they know when to start and stop each process. When there are two eyes they get the signal to stop making eyes.

Although scientists knew about chromosomes, they still did not have a clue as to how the magic-brick cells worked. But because this tiny group of 46 chromosomes in a human seemed to cause so many things to happen to make a person, they began to see that the chromosomes held the blueprint for life.

In 1909, Wilhelm Johannsen, a Danish botanist, who by then had read De Vries's work on heredity and the importance of the "factors," suggested that these factors be called "genes." This is from a Greek word that means "to give birth to," and the genes certainly give birth to many characteristics. Johannsen gave the name for the science of genetics.

In the early years of the twentieth century all branches of science were growing fast. As people began to learn about genetics they began to think that the only way all the different factors inherited could be explained was if each chromosome carried many separate factors, many separate genes.

But this theory had to be checked by experiments to prove or disprove it.

Thomas Hunt Morgan, an American born in Kentucky, was teaching experimental zoology at Columbia University in New York when he became involved in checking Gregor Mendel's laws of heredity with an amazing new tool.

In science it is not enough to come up with an idea. Ideas are everywhere. Nor is it enough to check an idea a few times. To become a fact, a theory must be tested and retested, over and over, until it is possible to predict an outcome every time, to say that if certain conditions exist, a predictable thing will happen. For example, when water is boiled at sea level, the liquid water changes to steam; when the temperature of water is reduced to 0 degrees Celsius, it changes from liquid to solid. Those are predictable facts.

Finding the right experiment and the right experimental animal or tool or model may often be the greatest part of the work. Mendel used sweet peas which took a year to grow and the entire experiment took years to complete. Morgan was looking for a living thing—plant or animal—that would allow him to see hundreds of generations quickly. He chose *Drosophila*, the fruit fly that flits around the fruit bowl so maddeningly every fall and that seems to come from nowhere.

The fruit fly became the new tool of genetics because it grows from egg to adult in only twelve days. Every two weeks there will be a new generation. It has only 8 chromosomes to work with, and these are large and easy to see. *Drosophila* also has unmistakable markings, such as a black body and short wings or a gray body and long wings.

In 1919, Morgan was ready to begin. He assembled hundreds of glass milk bottles and his flies. Then he got together his "fly squad," the dozens of graduate students who would feed the flies their banana mash and assist with experiments. Morgan ran his experiments for seventeen years, and of course the graduate students came and went, but the enthusiasm for the project never seemed to lag. Years after he left the project, one student wrote about it. "There can have been few times and places in scientific laboratories with such an atmosphere of excitement and such a record of sustained enthusiasm," he said.

That kind of enthusiasm can come only from a truly inspiring leader. Morgan was such a man, a good teacher, a person whose own fascination with the job spread to others. It could have been a boring, tedious job. Each of the thousands and thousands of fruit flies had to be examined with a hand lens, and precise records had to be kept for each tiny fly.

It was worth the work. From the millions of flies that grew in Morgan's fly rooms during those seventeen years, some very important facts were learned. First of all, Morgan proved conclusively that Gregor Mendel was right. The laws of heredity stood firm in spite of the fact that Mendel worked without any knowledge of chromosomes.

Next, Morgan showed that many traits are linked together,

inherited as a package deal, like red hair and freckles. Flies born with black bodies usually had short wings and flies with gray bodies usually had long wings. People with blond hair usually have blue eyes. The traits are linked together.

Then he discovered the secret of equal distribution of males and females in a population. The old wives' tales were not true in this regard. Every society has superstitions about how parents can produce a boy or a girl baby. Some say that the sex of a child can be influenced by looking at beautiful things if you want a girl or by eating certain foods if you want a boy. Morgan's experiments showed exactly how males and females have equal chances of distribution.

When Morgan looked at the fruit fly's chromosomes under the microscope, he saw that the female had one pair of chromosomes that looked like fat quotation marks made with the broad stroke of a pen. In the male that pair of chromosomes looked different; one of the pair was hooked at the end. Morgan called this the Y chromosome. From then on he referred to the male as having a pair of XY chromosomes and the female as having XX chromosomes.

Again, it was a simple matter of Mendelian assortment. Even distribution of males and females was assured by this XX and XY mating. The diagram on the next page shows that if an egg (XX) meets a sperm (XY) there is an equal number of chances that the offspring will have XX or XY.

This information led Morgan to discover that some traits are

The hereditary material of the fruit fly is contained in eight chromosomes. The male (*left*) has a hooked-shaped chromosome that determines the sex of the offspring.

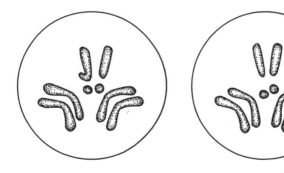

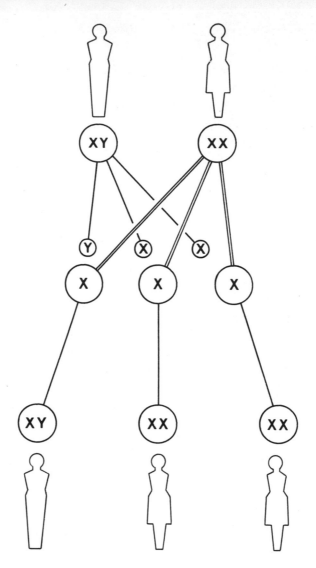

Distribution of XX XY chromosomes

sex-linked—that is, they are carried only on one sex gene or the other. This became vital information for genetic counseling when it is important to know whether the mother or father carries a disease.

Morgan's experiments never really stopped. They spread out and expanded as students started their own studies. Hermann Muller was one of Morgan's "fly squad" graduate students at Columbia after going to high school in the Bronx, where he was born. Muller was concerned about the way this almost invisible bit of matter, the chromosome, carried the instructions from parent to child.

No one had photographed a gene. They knew it was there from the way it behaved. The clues to it came from the things that happened from generation to generation. Muller thought that if they could hurry up these changes they might learn more. Changes are mutations, things like the appearance of a white-eyed fly among a batch of usually red-eyed flies. Mutations are rare. Morgan had waited a year for a white-eyed fly to show up.

Muller kept asking himself what made genes change. What caused mutations? He tried outside changes. If you cut off the tail of a mouse, all its offspring would still be born with tails. Muller tried drugs, motion, accidents of all kinds, but no mutations were produced.

Genes are well protected inside a body, in tissue, in a cell, in the cytoplasm (protoplasm outside the nucleus). From the information already gathered, Muller knew that genes are chemical compounds and that they might react to heat, which causes chemicals to change. There were a few results, a few mutations, but not enough to prove a theory. What could make one gene, a gene of the same chemical composition as one lying not a thousandth of a millimeter from it in the same cell, change when the others did not?

Muller began thinking of what he called "the world of the little." Perhaps mutations came from an ultramicroscopic accident. The gene could not escape a speeding electron. Muller knew then that radiation was the answer. Radiation from X-rays might cause experimental mutations. There is natural radiation in the atmosphere, which accounts for the rare natural mutation, and Muller decided to use large doses of X-rays to hurry the process.

In 1926, Muller and his own "fly squad" put hundreds of fruit flies into gelatin capsules and exposed them to varying amounts of X-rays. The X-rayed flies were then bred to untreated flies. In ten days, when the eggs from that mating hatched, Muller had the most amazing answer. There were thousands of flies, which he described as a "motley throng." He and his assistants could hardly believe what they saw under their hand lenses. There were flies with bulging eyes, flat eyes, dented eyes, purple eyes, yellow eyes, broad wings, curly wings, bumpy wings. Some were superactive, others almost dopy; some big, others tiny. When the statistics were in, Muller found that the X-rays had increased the number of mutations 150 times. His experiments were conclusive. He had repeated the experiments until he had raised seventy-five generations of fruit flies, which is equivalent to the generations of humans for twenty-five centuries.

Other scientists hurried to duplicate his work, using wasps, corn, Jimson weed. All found Muller to be right. Radiation causes mutation.

When Muller published his work in 1929, the great depression had hit the United States and money for research was limited. Then came World War II, which brought many changes in science. It also brought the nuclear bomb and radioactive fallout. Muller was alarmed. He knew that such fallout could do to all creatures what his X-rays did to *Drosophila*. He became an ardent opponent of nuclear bombs and joined with Albert Einstein and other scientists to have it banned. Scientists knew that too much exposure to X-rays can cause cancer, and Muller believed that cancer was a mutation, a change in the message to the cells so they no longer knew when to stop growing or changed in a disastrous way. He worked tirelessly to convince doctors not to use too much X ray in therapy or diagnosis.

Mutation is the key to evolution. Mutations are rare in nature, and most are damaging to the individual and add nothing to the species. Most mutants die. They cannot compete and so survive in their environment. An albino animal, for example, with no coloring in fur or feathers cannot hide from enemies, because it does not blend with its surroundings. A naturally white animal such as the polar bear in the Arctic, if born with dark fur as a mutation, would have the same survival problem. A predator, such as a hawk, if born with eyes that could not focus at a distance, would not survive long because it would not be able to find food.

Once in a while a change occurs in a gene that allows a species to improve just a bit, to adapt more easily, to live longer, to breed and pass on that mutated gene. Evolution is a series of such mutations over millions of years. But for every helpful change, there are many dangerous and damaging mutations. Muller feared that more radiation in the atmosphere from radioactive fallout would mean more of these damaging mutations. The years have proved him right.

After World War II, science became a different kind of race. No longer was it a relay, the picking up of the baton by one or two runners. Now it was a great marathon, in which all the runners were well trained, competitive, and had access to the same information published and shared worldwide. The splitting of the atom and the construction of the atom bomb had been an enormous team effort, a pooling of great scientists because it was truly a race against time. The pattern was set. Science had become more than ever a team game. People in different sciences began working together, too, overlapping into one another's specialties. Chemists worked with biologists, and physicists took on new importance as their work aided biology.

Physicists built the electron microscope and opened up a new world to the biologists. In a traditional microscope, light waves are focused by bending them through glass. In an electron microscope waves of electrons, which are shorter than waves of light, are bent or focused by magnetic fields.

Ernst Ruska, an electrical engineer in Germany, built the first crude electron microscope in 1932, before World War II. It could magnify 400 times, but it was a prototype and was not produced commercially. In 1937, before Americans turned all their efforts to the war, James Hillier, a Canadian physicist who became a United States citizen, improved the electron microscope so that it magnified 7,000 times.

Vladimir Zworkin, born in Russia and an American citizen by choice, was head of research at the great Radio Corporation of America (RCA). He developed the first television camera and then turned his attention to perfecting the electron microscope so that it could magnify 50,000 times. At last the inner workings of the cell could be seen, not just detected or suspected from the way the cell behaved. Today there are electron microscopes that magnify 2 million times. Now we can see a molecule, a large one, but still a molecule.

No longer are there men like Leeuwenhoek working in crude laboratories, untrained, without recognition, without assistance. The search for the blueprint of life has become big business—high-priority, heavily funded work with many men and women in on the search. The next step was to study nuclein, to discover what made the genes' magic bricks.

5 *The Model Builders*

The nuclein that Friedrich Miescher had put into jars was still on the shelves of the laboratory at the University of Strasbourg in 1879 when a young biochemist started his graduate work. Albrecht Kossel was taking a course in the relatively new science of biochemistry from Miescher's former teacher when he found the jars of nuclein. He began to analyze the material. He was curious about how its atoms were put together and how it worked.

First, he found that nuclein was a very large molecule made of two distinct parts. One part was protein and the other a non-protein so different from any other substance known that it was given the name nucleic acid to distinguish it from the rest of the nuclein.

When Kossel broke down the nucleic acids, he found that they were made of five different nitrogen-containing components: adenine, thymine, cytosine, guanine, and uracil. Adenine and guanine were large structures composed of two rings made of atoms of carbon, hydrogen, nitrogen, and oxygen. There were also other nitrogen components which were smaller and made of the same atoms in a single ring. The diagram shows this ring arrangement.

Diagram of nitrogen bases

1. A single ring representing cytosine
2. A double ring representing guanine

Kossel also found the presence of a sugar in the nucleic acid, but he could not isolate it. That part of nucleic acid was not identified until 1906, when Phoebus Levine at the Rockefeller Institute in New York put together more pieces of the puzzle. Levine and his team discovered that nucleic acid is actually a long chain of individual subunits which they called nucleotides. Each nucleotide consists of one of the nitrogen bases Kossel had found, a phosphate group, and a 5-carbon sugar.

There are many kinds of sugars. The sugar we eat is a 12-carbon sugar called sucrose, and the sugar used in hospitals for intravenous feedings is glucose, a 6-carbon sugar. Levine found that some nucleic acids contained the sugar ribose, a 5-carbon sugar, while others contained another 5-carbon sugar similar to ribose but lacking one oxygen atom. That sugar was called "deoxyribose."

The two nucleic acids were given names based on the difference in the sugars they contained. The one containing ribose was called ribonucleic acid (RNA), and the other deoxyribonucleic acid (DNA).

The diagram represents a nucleotide.

At last, the parts of the giant molecule, nuclein, were known. But once again it went back on the shelf.

A few years later, Robert Feulgen, a biochemist in Germany, was making some tests with a stain called acid fuchsin. Along with dozens of other substances, he stained some DNA, which turned a brilliant reddish-purple, a color often called fuchsia. He made note of the fact that the stain changed only DNA and filed it away to continue with other work.

In 1924, Feulgen put some of the fuchsin stain on living cells. The chromosomes, and only the chromosomes, turned bright fuchsia color as though he had suddenly lighted them with neon. Feulgen checked his earlier notes and found that only DNA had reacted in this way. The chromosomes were full of DNA, and no other part of the cell reacted to the stain.

It was the kind of test every scientist hopes to find—simple and conclusive. Quickly he tested living cells from all kinds of plants and animals, and the results were always the same. DNA showed up only in the chromosomes. From then on, in order to find whether DNA was present, the standard test became the Feulgen positive or negative reaction to acid fuchsin stain. It was foolproof and final. DNA was concentrated in the nucleus.

A biochemist in Berlin, Joachim Hammerling, did a series of experiments in 1931 with a tiny one-celled algae that proved that only the nucleus directed the cell's activities. More and more the evidence pointed to DNA as the blueprint of life.

The disagreement among scientists was over DNA versus the proteins as the blueprint of life. How could something made of only four subunits contain the code for all living things from elephants to amoeba? Proteins are much more complex and can be made up of as many as twenty different units. Maybe, argued many scientists, the DNA was only the "glue" that held the proteins together.

Although it is now obvious that DNA in the chromosomes is the part of the cell that carries the genetic messages, there were too many unknowns in the 1920s and early 1930s to make final statements. Facts were piling up as hunches were played and theories proved.

Two great laboratories went to work on the problem. At the University of Strasbourg and at the Rockefeller Institute in New York, a method for determining the amount of DNA in a cell was found. It turned out that the amount was constant for a species, just as the number of chromosomes for a species was constant. Proteins varied too much to fit the requirements for the carrier of hereditary traits.

But even with this evidence, scientists were cautious about making a blanket statement naming DNA as the one and only hereditary unit. They said, instead, that DNA is "closely associated" or that it is "most likely" the stuff of which genes are made. There had to be more proof, proof that was predictable.

While this DNA search was going on, a medical bacteriologist in England, Fred Griffith, was experimenting with bacteria to try to find how to control pneumonia. One strain of bacteria he used was called the S type because it appeared to have a smooth coat when seen under a microscope. The S type was virulent—that is, it caused pneumonia. The second type he called R because it had a rough coat. The R type was harmless. It did not cause pneumonia.

When Griffith injected mice with the S type bacteria, the mice got pneumonia, as he expected. When he injected other mice with the R type harmless bacteria, they did not, again as he expected. So far things went according to plan.

Next Griffith tried a method he thought might protect the mice against the pneumonia. A common way of making a vaccine against a disease is to inject a dead strain of the bacteria into the body and allow the body to build up its own antibodies, its own defenses, to fight the disease. Griffith killed some of the S type bacteria by boiling them. He injected some mice with this dead S type bacteria, and, as he expected, they did not get sick.

One day Griffith carried the experiment a step further. He injected a mouse with some of the dead S type bacteria and at the same time gave the same mouse some live R type bacteria. He did not expect the mouse to get sick because it had received no live, harmful, pneumonia-causing bacteria. He could hardly believe his eyes when the mouse got pneumonia. How could it?

To make sure he had not made a mistake, Griffith quickly injected many mice with both the dead S type and the live R type bacteria. All of them got pneumonia. He checked and rechecked his work. He examined the blood of the sick mice and found it full of living S type, pneumonia-causing bacteria. Somehow the live harmless bacteria had changed into pneumonia-causing bacteria.

Griffith took some of this transformed bacteria and made cultures of it in flasks. Then he saw what had happened. The S type bacteria, even though it had been killed by boiling, had passed along its S type information into the R type. Hereditary material from the dead bacteria had entered the live R cells and programmed them to act the same way as the dangerous bacteria!

Griffith's experiment with the S and R type bacteria

1. A mouse injected with harmless R type bacteria will not become sick.
2. A mouse injected with the S type, pneumonia-causing bacteria will get sick and die.
3. When the S type bacteria is boiled and killed and injected into a mouse, it will not kill the mouse because it is no longer harmful.
4. But when Griffith combined the R type harmless bacteria and the S type killed bacteria and injected it into a mouse . . .
5. . . . he expected the mouse to live.
6. Instead, the mouse died. Some genetic material from the dead S bacteria combined with genetic material from the live R bacteria, and the new combination caused the bacteria to be deadly. DNA had been exchanged.

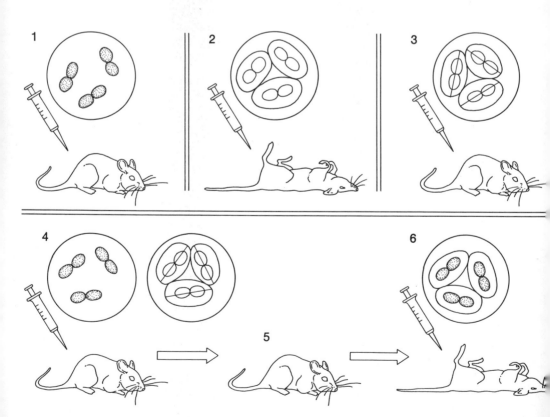

A substance had been transmitted that could withstand the killing of the cells in which it had started. One writer said that the scientists could not have been more astounded had a dog given birth to a cat.

Griffith's work was read avidly by other scientists in the 1920s and 1930s, but it was not until the 1940s that the real significance of his discovery became apparent. A group at the Rockefeller Institute, led by Oswald Avery, went one step further.

Avery and his team reworked all of Griffith's experiments with the pneumonia-causing bacteria, but this time they destroyed the DNA. Without the DNA, the bacteria could no longer pass along their genetic information. They proved beyond doubt that genes are DNA and DNA is genetic material. When we inherit a characteristic we have actually received a piece of DNA. In a way, the ancient beliefs were right. Although the mythical Adam and Eve did not hold the actual sperms or eggs for all of humanity to come, they did represent the genetic information for mankind.

The early 1950s brought a boom in babies, and in houses, cars, appliances, and other things that could not be had during the war. And scientists, with the horrors of atomic research fresh in their minds, turned to solving the key to life. There was enough information about the physical and chemical nature of DNA to make it the prize at the end of every laboratory's treasure hunt. Geneticists, biochemists, even physicists were brainstorming ways by which to unlock DNA's final secrets. And everyone was convinced that the secret must lie in the way in which it was built. It was a unique molecule, one which had to be able to duplicate itself over and over.

All the experiments and investigations sound simple in a brief telling, but of course they were not. They were extremely complicated. There were many dead ends, ideas scrapped, experiments started over.

A lot of the search for DNA makes one think of putting a jigsaw puzzle together. You can start by making the border or a corner, or perhaps with all the green pieces that look as though they will be a tree. Eventually you get the whole thing, but there is a lot of picking up and laying down of pieces, of trying to fit things in, sometimes even forcing them a little in the hope they will fit. Sometimes you hold the right piece in your hand, but because you are holding it upside down you don't see that it fits. That is an oversimplified way of explaining science, but it is the general idea. With the DNA search there was a lot of piece fitting going on in labs, a lot of starting at different places.

In the early 1950s, four people played leading roles in the drama of DNA, although dozens of others worked on its structure. Maurice Wilkins and Rosalind Franklin, chemical physicists at King's College at Cambridge University in England, combined crystallography, the study of crystals, with a technique called X-ray diffraction to get, not an exact picture of a substance, but an outline or "fingerprint" of it.

No electron microscope was powerful enough to see the DNA molecule, but with the X-ray diffraction, Wilkins and Franklin were able to learn a great deal about it. They passed X rays through crystals of DNA, and the beams of electrons produced a pattern on film.

It is something like the spatter prints that children make at camp by putting a leaf on paper and spattering paint over it with a toothbrush scrubbed over a screen. When the leaf is taken away a picture of the leaf does not appear but an outline does. From the outlines of the molecule and the shadows made by the X rays, physicists can make a mathematical analysis. From that they are able to build a three-dimensional model.

While Wilkins and Franklin worked on the X-ray diffraction at King's College, two other people were working at the Cavendish Laboratory, also at Cambridge. Francis Crick was an English physicist who had worked on radar and mine development during World War II and was anxious to become involved in biophysical research. James Watson was a twenty-four-year-old post-doctoral student from Chicago when he joined the group at Cavendish. After the discovery of the DNA molecular structure, Watson wrote a book, *The Double Helix*, about the people and events involved. In it he describes the excitement of those early postwar days of research, the feeling of adventure and hope that was in the air. "Sometimes I dreamed about discovering the secret of the gene," he reported, "but not once did I have the faintest trace of a respectable idea."

But Francis Crick did. He believed that if they could build a model of the molecule they could get some idea of how it was able to replicate—that is, to keep making copies of itself.

They knew the rules and the facts that they had to work with, the shapes of the pieces and the measurements of the molecules. They knew there were six pieces that had to fit together: adenine (A), guanine (G), cytosine (C), and thymine (T), which are the nitrogen bases, the sugar (deoxyribose), and the phosphate groups. They knew distances between the atoms and the angles of joining, and they also knew that the sugar and phosphate pieces formed long, regular chains.

The DNA molecule is extremely long, a thousand times longer than it is wide. If you magnified a cell so that you could barely see it as a tiny dot, the DNA coiled in its nucleus would stretch out the length of a football field.

While Watkins and Crick mulled over ways to build the molecule, Wilkins and Franklin worked on it as their major project at King's College. Wilkins had worked with the Americans on the atomic-bomb project during the war, and he was anxious to put that behind him, as were most of the scientists involved in that research. He turned his attentions to solving the DNA problem with X-ray diffraction. Rosalind Franklin, who joined him, was a talented young crystallographer. She and Wilkins took an instant dislike to each other, which was unfortunate for their work. Had they been compatible and shared their progress, they might have found the key to DNA before Watson and Crick did. As it was, they supplied valuable information that verified Watson's and Crick's model.

In California, Linus Pauling, one of the world's leading chemists, had been studying the structure of some protein molecules and had built a model of one of them. The model was like a spiral staircase, a single helix. Watson and Crick studied that report and realized that Pauling had found the solution to his problem not by looking at X rays but by playing with models, by asking "which atoms like to sit next to each other." This reinforced their determination to build a DNA model.

The problem was always on their minds. They doodled, dreamed of it, and discussed it after parties, between tennis games, over coffee. When a scientist, or any creative person, is staring out the window or leaning back in a chair with his feet on the desk he may be doing his best work. Thinking. Mulling it over. Daydreaming.

Then the head of the Cavendish Laboratory took Watson and Crick off the DNA project, pointing out that the DNA problem belonged to Wilkins and Franklin, that they had started work on it first. But, Watson reported, "the moratorium on working on DNA did not extend to thinking about it."

A year went by and Watson and Crick turned their attention to other projects. But they did not put DNA out of their minds. "The idea of genes being immortal smelled right," said Watson, and he knew they were on the right track.

One of the problems that had to be solved was the arrangement of the long coil of sugar and phosphates that scientists called the backbone. To this backbone would be attached all the pieces of A,T,C, and G. There was great disagreement. Some thought the backbone should be on the inside of the model, and the first one that was built was wrong.

In 1953, Linus Pauling produced a model of DNA, and Watson and Crick practically held their breaths waiting to see what it was. When they read the report they knew the model was wrong. Pauling had built a three-chain helix with the sugar-phosphate backbone in the center.

When they started their investigation, Watson and Crick had also thought the sugar-phosphate backbone should be in the center, but evidence was piling up that this was not the case.

Watson saw that Pauling's mistake was one of simple college chemistry, an error in calculation that had not been caught. He was convinced that it would not take Pauling long to realize this mistake and correct it. He figured that, with any luck, he and Crick might have a six-week lead. He went to King's college, where Rosalind Franklin, discouraged by the reactions to her work, was getting ready to move to another research lab. Maurice Wilkins showed Watson the newest X-ray diagrams that Rosalind Franklin had made. They were overwhelming evidence for a helix with the sugar-phosphate backbone on the outside. Her notes, too, show that her evidence was correct:

"The results suggest a helical structure (which must be very closely packed) containing probably 2, 3, or 4 co-axial nucleic acid chains per helical unit, and having the phosphate groups near the outside."

Watson hurried back to Cavendish and got permission from the head of the laboratory to return to the DNA project with Crick. They were convinced that when they found the DNA molecule, it would be not only simple, but beautiful as well.

They asked the metal shop to make flat tin pieces in the shapes of the four nitrogen bases, A,T,C, and G. They gathered wire and clamps and began playing with pieces, following the rules that told them which atoms would fit with which others.

At one point they were sure they had found the answer by using two coils of the backbone connected by equal parts of each of the bases so that it looked like the diagram below.

They had built it so that there was like with like; an A equaled an A, and a G equaled a G. Then they remembered that Erwin Chargaff, an Austrian-born biochemist, had published a paper in America in 1949, pointing out that in the DNA molecule there is always an equal amount of adenine and thymine $(A = T)$ and an equal amount of cytosine and guanine $(C = G)$. Like equals like could not be the answer. It did not fit the proven facts, the evidence of experimentation.

Back to fiddling around with the pieces. One day while Watson was picking up the pieces shaped like the bases, exactly as one picks up a piece of a jigsaw puzzle and turns it different ways, he saw that when he put together an adenine and thymine pair, they

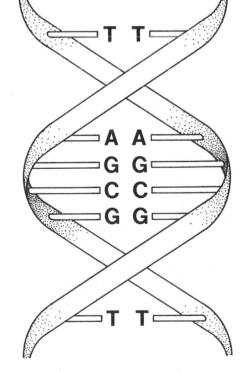

Watson and Crick's first model of DNA was a helix in which the nucleotides were like matched with like: adenine matched with adenine and quanine matched with quanine, for example.

were exactly the same shape as a pair of guanine-cytosine. That was it! The answer fitted Chargaff's rules. The model could work only if the bases were in that exact pairing. It could work only as a double helix, a beautiful, simple staircase in which the steps were the pairs of nitrogen bases.

The model was crude and wobbly, held together with wire, and some of the parts were stiff cardboard because the shop had been slow supplying the metal pieces. But to Watson and Crick it was magnificent.

James D. Watson (*on the left*) and Francis Crick with a model of DNA that they built from cardboard, wire, and metal. (The Bettmann Archive)

Checking with Maurice Wilkins, they soon knew that their model fitted the facts of the X-ray diffraction analysis. They decided to make a joint announcement. It was a one-page article in the April 25, 1953, issue of the British magazine *Nature*. With great understatement it began, "We wish to suggest a structure . . . for the salt of DNA."

A Nobel prize was awarded to Watson, Crick, and Wilkins in 1962. Rosalind Franklin, who had died, at the age of thirty-seven, before it was presented, did not share in the credit for the discovery.

There was still a great deal to be done to prove that the structure of DNA was what the model suggested it to be. This was, after all, only a model, only a suggestion pieced together from accumulated facts and incredible imagination. No one had seen a DNA molecule or measured one. But it looked as though this was it.

Now, how did it work? How did this beautiful double helix supply information to all living things?

6

Alphabets and Zippers

Like the color of my skin on the day that I grow old,
My life is made of patterns that can scarcely be controlled.
Paul Simon, "Patterns"

The initials DNA became as familiar as FBI or CIA. After Watson and Crick built the model, scientists went all out to find the proof. If they could synthesize DNA, make it in the laboratory, put it together, and take it apart again, they would know they had found the key to life.

They knew that DNA was an alphabet with four letters. The letters make up the genes, which are sentences strung out end to end on the chromosomes. A bacterium has about 2,000 genes and each gene has about 1,000 letters or links. The bacterium's DNA is about 2 million letters.

The DNA humans carry is more than 1 billion letters, equal to 10,000 novels of 100,000 words each. The miracle is in the transcribing of these letters. How many pages of a book can be copied without a mistake? DNA copies and copies and copies, with mistakes so rare, with mutations so few, that it is almost unbelievable.

When Watson and Crick were looking for the structure of DNA they were sure it would be both simple and beautiful. It is.

DNA has two functions. First, it is responsible for the continuity of heredity. One cell divides to form two cells, and each new cell has the identical DNA. A human being starts as a single cell, and that cell divides until each person contains 60,000 billion cells, each with the same DNA, the same blueprint.

The second function of DNA is to send instructions to the cells so that each does what it is supposed to do.

The first function is easier to explain and understand. Picture DNA as a ladder, with the phosphates and sugars as the side rails and the nitrogen bases as the rungs. Each nitrogen base is attached to a side rail and bonded in the middle with its opposite nitrogen base. The nitrogen bases follow Chargaff's rule; only A bonds with T and only G with C. If the phosphate, sugar, and nitrogen-base ladder is given a half twist, the result is the double helix.

The bonds that hold the A and T and the G and C together are relatively weak. When a cell is ready to divide to form two equal cells, the DNA molecules unzip. The bonds holding A and T or C and G break. If a ladder was cut in half by sawing through the middle of each rung, that would show how DNA works.

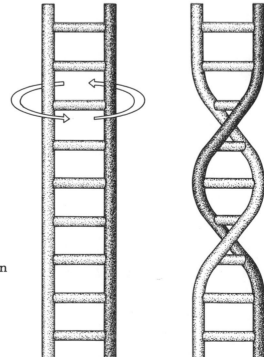

The double helix construction of DNA is like a ladder that is twisted.

Unzipped, the DNA molecule is two separate strands. Other nucleotides, phosphate, the sugar deoxyribose, and nitrogen bases produced in the cytoplasm of the cell now begin to fit into the unzipping molecule, each always matching its opposite part. Where there had been one strand of DNA, there are now two. Each half of the ladder has acted like a pattern, called a template, for the building of its new half.

Now there is an exact strand of DNA to go to each of the new cells when the cell divides. Both cells will have exactly the same heredity material, identical DNA. It is a simple way of providing the blueprint that makes sure that human mothers give birth to human babies and not kittens, or elephants produce elephants and not dogs.

The second function of DNA is more complex. DNA carries the code for all the instructions for the cell, yet it never leaves the cell. Somehow it must send messages into the cytoplasm, where the

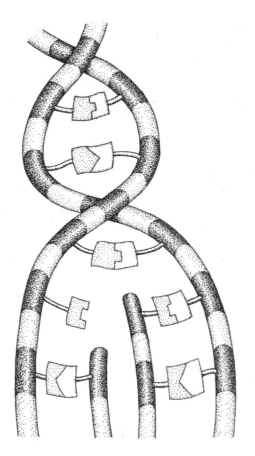

Replication of DNA

Where there was one strand of DNA, now there are two. Each half of the ladder has acted like a pattern for the building of a new half.

activity takes place. Every cell has to have instructions for making the materials it needs to repair or reproduce itself. A glandular cell in the pancreas needs the blueprint for making insulin. A cell in the bone marrow needs the plans for making hemoglobin for the red blood cells.

An instruction manual for operating a transcontinental 747 jet or the computer system of a bank fills hundreds of pages. The instruction manual for building a model plane is bigger than the genetic plans for building a blue whale. And the plane cannot repair itself or reproduce.

Each cell in the body gets its instructions from this microscopic bit of DNA, even though a muscle cell differs from a skin cell or a liver cell. The differences in the cells depend upon the proteins the cell is programmed to produce. Insulin is a protein, a large part of hemoglobin is protein, and most of the active part of a muscle is protein.

An animal also contains carbohydrates, minerals, some fats and oils, but the largest part, other than water, is protein. A dog's fur, skin, and muscle are primarily protein. People move and think and see with protein. In every cell of the body countless chemical reactions are taking place every second, and none of these reactions could happen without protein. The special proteins that make these reactions take place are called enzymes. They are important and we hear about them a lot.

Enzymes are needed to make complex sugars out of simple sugars, to make fats and oils, and to digest food and release energy. Every reaction in the body requires one or more enzymes.

Some scientists estimate that a human being is composed of over 100,000 different proteins. The kinds of proteins a living creature contains and the way the proteins are put together determine what the living thing will be—an amoeba, a lion, or a maple tree.

One of the best descriptions of the way to understand the proteins of living things was written by Dr. Mahlon B. Hoagland and it is worth repeating. He compares the proteins to the metal of a car. There are many different materials in a car, but the main substance is metal. The metal determines what the car looks like and how it operates. The metal's shape, quality, and position of its parts determine how one car differs from another.

The DNA in the cell provides codes for the many proteins. It resembles the Morse code, which has two symbols, but the DNA code has four units, A, T, C, and G. The dot and dash of the Morse code can send an enormous variety of messages. The nitrogen-base code can send hundreds and hundreds of thousands of messages. Different parts of the DNA molecule will code for protein. Each of those parts may be made up of hundreds of units, each unit a gene.

When a certain protein is needed by a cell, the part of the DNA containing the code for that protein unzips. Then RNA, the other nucleic acid, acts as the messenger. The RNA copies DNA's code and carries it to the cytoplasm and to structures called ribosomes. The ribosomes are protein factories. RNA is similar to DNA, except it has only one strand—half the ladder, and it contains the sugar ribose instead of deoxyribose. It has four bases. Three of them are exactly the same as those of DNA: adenine, guanine, and cytosine. The fourth is different. Instead of thymine, RNA contains the base uracil.

The messenger RNA uses the unzipped part of DNA as a pattern. If the code of DNA is AGCCT, the RNA forms the opposite code that fits into it, UCGGA.

Carrying this code, the RNA leaves the nucleus and goes out

The formation of messenger RNA using the unzipped part of DNA as a pattern

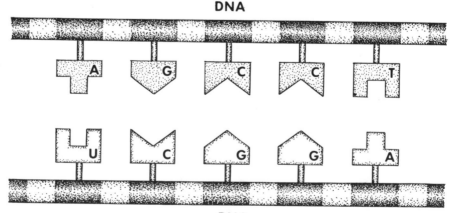

to the protein-factory ribosomes. There are thousands of ribosomes in a cell's cytoplasm and they produce thousands of proteins.

A DNA chain is made up of nucleotides, but a protein is a long chain molecule made up of amino acids. There are twenty different amino acids which are called the building blocks of proteins. The kinds of amino acids and the sequence in which they are arranged determine the kind of protein to be made. Generally, one gene determines one protein.

The RNA approaches the ribosome with the opposite code it has made from the DNA pattern, and with this code it tells the ribosome what amino acids to put together to make the protein needed. How do these amino acids know in what sequence to arrange themselves to become the protein?

Francis Crick thought about that after he and Watson put together the structure of DNA, and he became fascinated with the problem. He had stayed at Cambridge, and he and a team of other scientists came up with the theory that there must be a second kind of RNA in the cytoplasm, a go-between from the amino acids to the RNA. Crick called it an adaptor molecule.

In 1956, two American biochemists, Hoagland and Paul Zamecnik, found the presence of just such an adaptor molecule. They called it "transfer RNA," written as tRNA. The tRNA attaches itself to a specific amino acid and puts it in the right place opposite the messenger RNA (mRNA). Other tRNAs carrying their amino acids place them in the proper position according to the code. This proper sequence of amino acids produces the protein ordered by the DNA.

All this, which takes so long to explain, happens in a fraction of a second, and the process is repeated in every cell of the body continually from the time an organism begins as a fertilized egg until it dies.

The next question that puzzled the scientists was how many of these nitrogen bases determined the code for DNA. They knew there must be a code but they did not know the code. It was like knowing that dot and dash are the Morse code, but not knowing how to put the dots and dashs together to make letters. Again, Francis Crick, the idea man, took mathematical evidence and in 1961 proposed the theory that each amino acid was coded by three nitrogen bases.

It did not take long for experimental evidence to prove him

right. The code of life is a triplet code, a code using the letters A, G, C, and T, in groups of three. When this triplet code is transposed to the RNA, it uses the letters A, G, C, and U; the U is for uracil, which replaces the T for thymine in the DNA codes. These are also used in groups of three. Groups of three nitrogen bases provide more than enough combinations to code for the twenty amino acids.

This is how it works: One of the amino acids is valine. Valine's code is GUA. Its opposite code on the transfer RNA must be CAU because that is the only one that will fit. Only GUA will place valine in the right position to make the protein molecule of which it is part. Arginine, another amino acid, is coded by the bases CGC. Its opposite code on the transfer RNA must be the only one that will fit, GCG.

Like so many of the laws of nature, the key to the code of life turned out to be simple and beautiful.

After the code was known, hundreds of investigations began, which eventually found all the code letters for the amino acids, producing a "dictionary" of the code of life.

While many biochemists worked on the codes, others were curious about the ways in which hereditary material was passed along. For a long while it was thought that DNA was passed from cell to cell only during fertilization, when a sperm joined an egg, or during cell division, when one cell made two daughter cells.

But after Griffith's experiments with the pneumonia-causing bacteria and the mice showed that hereditary material was passed on in another way, a new series of investigations began. Suddenly the virus became very important.

A virus is a "thing" that most scientists agree exists in some twilight zone between animals and minerals. Some call it the "largest molecule," and others say it is the "smallest organism." It comes in a variety of shapes from rods to tadpoles, but it always has an outer coat made of protein, and inside this is nucleic acid, either DNA or RNA but not both. A virus grows in the way a mineral crystal grows, but it is a parasite that can only live inside a cell. It always carries disease.

A Dutch botanist, Martinus Beijerinck, named the virus in 1898 when he was looking for the cause of a disease that stunted the growth and spotted the leaves of the tobacco plant. He knew it wasn't caused by bacteria, but whatever it was escaped through his

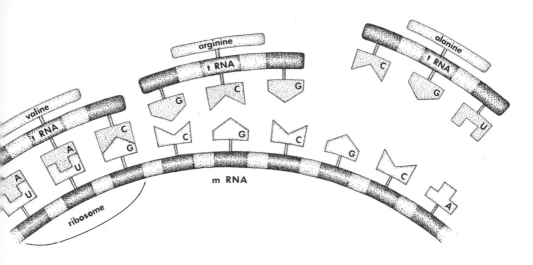

The production of protein

The triplet code of the transfer RNA is specific for an amino acid and places the amino acid in the correct order to become a protein.

finest filters. He called it the filterable virus and he thought it was a liquid. "Virus" is from the Latin word for poison.

The tobacco mosaic virus, commonly called TMV, is considered the "granddaddy of the viruses," because it was the first one identified, purified, crystallized, taken apart, and put together again. It has taught us a lot about life processes. In 1935, an American chemist, Wendell Stanley (who started out to be a football coach before he got interested in chemistry), caused heated controversy when he produced the first crystals of TMV. People argued over whether viruses were living or non-living. How could something be alive if crystals could be made of it, and how could it be mineral if it reproduced itself?

A British bacteriologist, Frederick Twort, had identified a "bacteria-eating" virus in 1915. This was a kind of virus that entered a bacteria, took it over and killed it, while reproducing itself. It was called a "bacteriophage."

A bacteriophage looks like a miniature moon-landing craft with a boxlike head. The head is packed with spirals of DNA. It has a tail that works like the needle of a syringe and is surrounded by spider-like legs. The phage, as it is commonly called, lands on a living bacterial cell. It injects its DNA into the cell and immediately takes over control of the cell machinery. It sends signals to

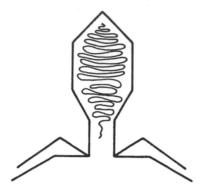

A bacteria-eating virus called a bacteriophage. Its head is full of DNA.

the cell's protein-making centers to stop making bacterial protein and start making virus protein. In a matter of minutes, the cell is building new heads, tails, DNA, and legs for new viruses. Under the electron microscope this process can be seen. When about 100 of these new viruses are assembled, they then secrete an enzyme which destroys the outer membrane of the bacterium. The viruses burst out, leaving a dead cell. The entire invasion takes less than half an hour.

Researchers were greatly interested in this virus injection method of passing along hereditary information, and other investigations began to find out other ways in which genes might be transmitted.

In 1952, two young American biochemists, Joshua Lederberg and Norton Zinder, working with the bacteriophages, discovered that genetic information could be carried by viruses from one type of bacterium to another.

They found that a piece of DNA from the host bacterium sometimes gets mixed up with the DNA of the virus, and the newly made virus actually carries away with it a fragment of the bacterial chromosome. It adds this stolen bit of DNA to another newly infected bacterium, which from that time on carries a new hereditary trait. This new trait becomes a permanent change, a regular part of the message of its genes, a "gift" from a strange bacterium by courtesy of an invading virus.

This method in which bits of DNA from one living thing recombine with bits of DNA from another living thing is called transduction. It was such an exciting and vital piece of information that it earned researchers Nobel prizes and interested other researchers in digging further into the subject.

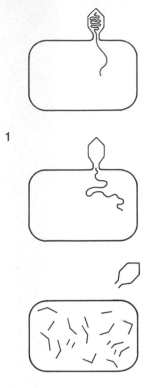

1

2

1. The bacteriophage injects its DNA into the bacterium.
2. Inside the cell, the virus's DNA takes over and orders the cell's protein-making factory to make pieces of virus.
3. When about 100 of these new viruses appear, their newly formed heads full of virus DNA, they secrete an enzyme that destroys the bacterium's membrane. The new viruses escape.

3

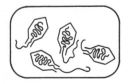

Every living thing is a chemical factory, a superorganized series of actions and reactions, following rules that do not vary. If living things such as bacteria could receive bits of stolen DNA, would it not be possible for higher forms of life to operate in the same way? Perhaps viruses were carriers of bits of DNA from human to human, DNA that might be coded to signal cells to lose control, to become cancerous. Perhaps DNA could be deliberately recombined to create useful enzymes or even other organisms.

With the secret of the structure of DNA revealed, and the method of how it was passed along beginning to be understood, some scientists began to think about ways in which they could use these rules of nature to work for man. Perhaps they could not create life, but it was beginning to look as though they might be able to change it.

7 *Playing God*

The first of a batch of two hundred and fifty embryonic
rocket-plane engineers was just passing the eleven hundred
metre mark on Rack 3. A special mechanism kept their
containers in constant rotation. "To improve their sense of
balance," Mr. Foster explained. "Doing repairs on the
outside of a rocket in mid-air is a ticklish job. We slacken
off the circulation when they're right way up, so that they're
half-starved, and double the flow of surrogate when they're
upside down. They learn to associate topsy-turvydom with
well-being; in fact, they're only truly happy when they're
standing on their heads.

Aldous Huxley, *Brave New World*

Brave New World is a great science-fiction novel that suggested
baby factories by 1980. We are a long way from that, and we will
not be likely to have the kind of assembly lines Huxley imagined.
We have other methods of bio-engineering, methods not as drastic,
dramatic, or dehumanizing as those of Huxley's world.

As a matter of fact, people were engineering living things long
before the genetic code was broken. When man began to domesti-

cate animals, he engineered which ones would be allowed to breed, selecting the gentlest dog or the fastest horse or the cow that gave the most milk. Royal families even selected humans for intermarriage, unfortunately passing along the genes for such defects as hemophilia, the bleeding disease.

In nature, species do not interbreed. A gorilla does not mate with a chimpanzee, a dog does not mate with a cat, an owl with a hawk, or a frog with a salamander.

When species are mixed in mating and an odd animal is produced, the offspring is sterile. It cannot breed and pass along those mixed genes. Lions and tigers have been interbred at zoos, resulting in a tiglon or a liger, but the result is forever its own family. A female horse bred with a male donkey will produce a mule, but mules are sterile. If a farmer wants a young mule, he again must breed a horse and a donkey. We have not successfully mingled the genes of species, to change them, to alter evolution.

Until now.

Now we have reached the level of biology where we can cross a bacterium with a plant, an animal, other bacteria, or a virus. We can mix and match, create new life forms, and it is scary. We are asking scientists and scientists are asking one another, "Is it worth the risks?"

Genetic engineering is here to stay. When scientists were unlocking the secrets of the atom, there was much fear, well-founded fear. They produced horror. Since then, however, from the knowledge that built the atomic bomb has come products and services that make life better for man.

Now we are taking the gamble that the information found in life's inner secrets will pay off in better health, more food, and better environmental conditions for all living things. Since the beginning of the earth, probably more than 5 billion years ago, evolution has been slow, so slow that it is impossible to imagine. By continual reshuffling of the genetic cards, through much trial and error, today's life forms have evolved. Now we are rushing evolution, creating new species in a day, and scientists are choosing sides over whether the gamble is worth taking.

The new biology brings to some minds the threat of monsters, plagues, and superhuman creatures. It is possible that an error, or a deliberate act, could cause a worldwide epidemic by newly created bacteria or trigger a catastrophe by unbalancing the ecology. Some people fear that terrorists may create a virus or a disease that will wipe out nations and give them the power to dominate and control the human spirit.

Good or evil is the choice that goes with every discovery.

Genetic engineering may one day eliminate horrible genetic defects. It may produce healing drugs and hormones, and it may allow us to conquer cancer.

The experiments that are causing the arguments are with a technique called recombinant DNA. It is a kind of experiment in which bits of DNA of one species are blended or recombined with the DNA of another. In each case a new organism is created, one with a new blueprint, and we have no way of predicting how it will behave.

For Mendel the experimental animal was the sweet pea, for Morgan it was the fruit fly. For recombinant DNA it is *E. coli*, proper name *Escherichia coli*, a bacterium a ten-thousandth of an inch long. It is named after the German pediatrician who isolated the bacteria in 1885. *E. coli* is found commonly in the human colon, and it is a marvelous experimental animal because it is so well known and because it produces an entire generation in 20 minutes.

In the recombinant experiments, the *E. coli* is put in a test tube with a detergentlike liquid which dissolves the outer membrane. The DNA then spills out of the bacteria. Most of it is in a long strand, but some of the DNA is contained in small, closed loops called plasmids. Each plasmid has only a few genes.

These plasmids are known to pick up genes from other plasmids or from the bacterial chromosomes. They can carry the picked-up DNA with them to a new cell, and they move in and out of bacteria easily. The biologists are using this ability of the plasmids to transport foreign DNA.

The plasmids are separated from the long strands of chromosomal DNA in a piece of equipment called a centrifuge. Test tubes are placed in the centrifuge and spun around until all the heavier material, like the plasmids, drops to the bottom of the test tube. The plasmids collected in this way are put into a chemical called a restriction enzyme, a special protein that cuts the plasmids open, leaving the open plasmids with "sticky ends."

The open plasmids with their sticky ends are then mixed with the genes, the bits of DNA, which have been taken from another bacterium, a virus, a plant, or an animal. In this mixture is another enzyme, one called DNA ligase, a kind of glue for DNA. It glues the new gene onto the sticky ends of the open plasmid and a new loop is formed, a new creature, one whose blueprint has been changed. The loop of changed plasmid is now called a chimera. (Chimera was the name given by the Greeks to a mythical animal of several parts—lion, goat, and serpent.)

When these chimeras are put into a solution of calcium chloride with normal *E. coli* and heated, the new plasmid chimeras penetrate the *E. coli*. They enter the bacteria and become part of the genetic blueprint of the *E. coli*. When *E. coli* divides itself, copies of the new plasmid are also made.

Why go to all this trouble to change a gene or two? What good does it do? The first and right now one of the most important reasons for these experiments is to be able to map the genes, to know what gene is where and what each gene does.

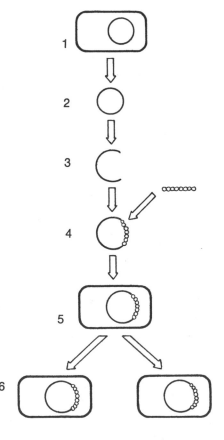

How DNA is recombined

1. A cell of *E. coli* with a plasmid inside. The outer membrane is dissolved.
2. A plasmid spills out.
3. The plasmid is cut open with a special protein, leaving sticky ends.
4. DNA from another cell or a virus is "glued" into place with another enzyme.
5. The plasmid re-enters a bacterium.
5. When the *E. coli* divides, copies of the new plasmid are copied, too.

Of all the hundreds and thousands of genes carried on the forty-six human chromosomes, only three or four have been identified. If human genes could be transplanted one at a time into *E. coli* and replicated, it would be possible to map all the genes.

With that information we might be able to understand the molecular basis of cancer. Many scientists feel that cancer is basically the cell's genetic machinery gone haywire. Cells that had fully developed suddenly get a signal to start again and they do not stop. Cancerous cells grow uncontrollably. Discovering the way to control cancer would be reason enough for recombinant DNA experiments.

Knowledge of the genes would allow us to do something about inherited defects. The National Foundation–March of Dimes reports that more than 2,000 genetic diseases have been identified and none of them can be cured. A birth defect, or genetic disease, is defined by that organization as an "abnormality of structure, function, or metabolism genetically determined or the result of environmental influence on the unborn child." Birth defects range from crooked teeth and defective blood cells to missing limbs and diseases that kill. Every year in the United States more than 250,000 babies are born with one or more defects.

A group of defects that are always found together is called a syndrome. Down's syndrome is an example. It used to be called mongolism and it is a combination of mental retardation and physical defects. Down's syndrome is the result of an extra chromosome —forty-seven chromosomes instead of the usual forty-six. The only thing that can be done about it at present is genetic counseling, advice to prospective parents after blood tests have shown the extra chromosome. If we could re-engineer the genes, it might be possible to correct the extra chromosome.

Other genetic defects include color blindness, deafness, muscular dystrophy, glaucoma, sickle-cell anemia, and hemophilia, none of which can be cured. Some can be corrected surgically, others can be controlled by special diet or drugs, but for some there is no treatment.

A disease called phenylketonuria (PKU) is an example of a genetic disease that is controlled. It is caused by the inability of the body to metabolize a specific amino acid. Dr. Robert Guthrie at the Children's Hospital in Buffalo, N.Y., identified the cause of this disease, which, if not treated, leaves a child mentally retarded. Dr.

Guthrie found that children given a special diet soon after birth could overcome the effects of the disorder. This is not a cure, but a treatment. It is so effective that most states now have laws requiring that a newborn infant be tested for PKU. Some day, when the

When a human cell in the process of dividing is placed under a microscope, the 46 chromosomes can be seen clearly. (Medical Genetics Unit, Dept. of Medicine, State University of N.Y. at Buffalo)

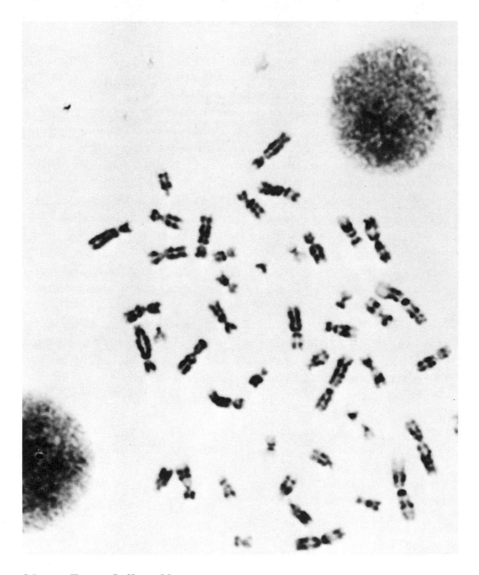

CHROMOSOME ANALYSIS

7C	Phenotypic sex female	Lab no. & Pedigree 36/274
ding	Chromosome count this cell:	46
	Date:	
normalities this cell: none	Banded: Trypsin-Giemsa	
46,XX		

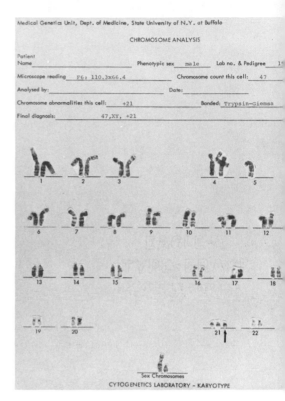

Medical Genetics Unit, Dept. of Medicine, State University of N.Y. at Buffalo

CHROMOSOME ANALYSIS

Patient
Name _____ Phenotypic sex male Lab no. & Pedigree 1

Microscope reading F6: 110.3x66.4 Chromosome count this cell: 47

Analysed by: _____ Date: _____

Chromosome abnormalities this cell: +21 Banded: Trypsin-Giemsa

Final diagnosis: 47,XY, +21

Sex Chromosomes
CYTOGENETICS LABORATORY - KARYOTYPE

(*Left*) When the photographs of the human chromosomes are cut apart and pasted on a form like this, the pairs of chromosomes are matched and abnormalities become apparent. This is a normal karyotype. (Medical Genetics Unit, State University of N.Y. at Buffalo)

(*Right*) This is the karyotype of a person who carries an extra gene. With this extra Number 21 gene, the person will be mentally retarded and carry physical defects of the Down's Syndrome, previously known as mongolism. (Medical Genetics Unit, State University of N.Y. at Buffalo)

genes have been mapped and it is known how they work, it might be possible to correct this defect, to alter the gene before the child is born.

Chromosomal defects are often a combination of heredity and environment, especially when the environment of the embryo has been altered by radiation or pollutants. There is conclusive evidence that children born to women who have a steady diet of fish contaminated by mercury are likely to be brain-damaged. Excessive radiation, even from repeated diagnostic X-rays of some kinds, will cause mutations in the genes of humans as it did in the fruit flies.

Few people would think it necessary to create the perfect person, the person with perfect teeth, perfect skin, perfect eyes, "perfect" mentality. Individual differences are what make people interesting. But if genetic engineering could take away the pain and sorrow of those afflicted by crippling disorders, it would be worth certain risks.

When the recombinant DNA experiments began in the early 1970s, some scientists began to worry. They wondered what would happen if a dangerous, disease-causing bacteria were produced that would get into the human gut and grow there as easily as *E. coli* does. What if a cancer-producing virus or a disease for which there was no natural defense accidentally got out of the laboratory? There was fear of a biological Hiroshima.

"Have we the right to counteract, irreversibly, the evolutionary wisdom of millions of years, in order to satisfy the ambition and the curiosity of a few scientists? The future will curse us for it," said Dr. Erwin Chargaff in a letter to the journal *Science*, published by the American Association for the Advancement of Science.

Dr. Chargaff had done important work on the structure of DNA and when a scientist of the ability and wisdom of Chargaff wonders, the scientific community takes notice. Geneticists in 1973 called a moratorium on genetic experiments while they discussed the question among themselves. Most agreed that since nature has been recombining DNA molecules for millions of years, the danger lies not in the recombining itself, but in the choice of molecules to be spliced.

"Hybrids that aren't natural are the scary ones," said one scientist.

In 1975, a conference took place in Asilomar, California. It was an international meeting of more than 100 biologists, some lawyers, and reporters. They argued, fought, and thought, and when it was over, the conference suggested some guidelines that all researchers in genetics should follow. These were not laws. The National Institutes of Health (NIH), from which most money comes for genetic research, published the list of rules to be followed by anyone who wants to get grant money for experiments.

The rules specify that some experiments would absolutely not be done at all. No one, for example, might transplant genes from a high-risk, disease-causing organism.

Two kinds of control were described, one called physical containment and the other biological containment. Physical containment regulated the way a laboratory should be built and maintained. The NIH's code ranges from P-1, which is a standard biology laboratory with the usual sterile conditions and safeguards, to P-4, which has the greatest restrictions. The first P-4 lab was built at the NIH's building 550 at Fort Detrick, Maryland, and it is more secure than NASA's Lunar Receiving Laboratory, which was built when it was thought that astronauts might return from the moon with dangerous "bugs."

Workers entering a P-4 lab must wear special protective coveralls and must walk through an air lock. To leave, even for lunch, workers must walk through the air lock, strip off the coveralls, and shower. The materials used are never touched. The workers use "glove boxes," which are glass-fronted stainless-steel boxes fitted with shoulder-length gloves that the workers put their arms into.

Any materials that leave a P-4 lab pass through a steam sterilizer and a disinfectant bath. Even the air goes through an incinerator before it goes outside. In addition to all these precautions, the rules for biological containment specify that the only *E. coli* used for the experiments should be a special weakened strain that cannot survive outside the medium it is grown in.

At the Asilomar conference, a geneticist, Roy Curtiss III, volunteered to "build" a variety of *E. coli* that would not be able to survive outside the lab, a tailor-made microbe that could not colonize or live in the human intestine. His *E. coli* is easily destroyed by common household detergents. It is absolutely safe, but it still provides the perfect experimental animal for gene-splicing. Curtiss named it *E. coli* × 1776, in honor of the bicentennial year in which he did the work.

There are so many benefits to genetic engineering that they seem to outweigh the hazards. Tailoring information to fit into defective genes or inserting new genes to replace scrambled genes would be reason enough for continuing the research. But there are other advantages, not only in medicine but in industry and agriculture.

It will be possible to custom-build bacteria to work as miniature factories to produce important drugs, hormones, and other medicines quickly and cheaply. Insulin is produced normally by the pancreas, but when there is a defect so the gene does not send the insulin-producing information, the disease called diabetes is the result. Diabetics are treated with injections of insulin extracted from cattle and pigs. About 5 percent of diabetics are allergic to the animal-produced insulin.

When the insulin-producing gene is spliced into *E. coli*, the *E. coli*'s DNA reading machinery will produce insulin that has many advantages. It will be quality-controlled, the same every time. It is fast, because the bacteria double their number every twenty minutes, and it is cheap, because you don't need stables to raise bacteria. Insulin production by bacteria is not yet an assembly-line procedure, but it will be in a few years.

Researchers isolating the hormone somatostatin from the brains of animals for tests used brains from half a million sheep to produce 5 milligrams (0.00018 ounce). With re-engineered genes, gallons of somatostatin can be produced by bacteria in a lab.

Industry, too, is finding uses for gene-spliced bacteria. At the U.S. Army laboratory in Natick, Massachusetts, an enzyme that will digest wood has been isolated. This enzyme spliced into bacteria can be put to work digesting the large molecules of cellulose from old newspapers, wood chips, and even cow dung. The product of the digestion is sugar, which can then be fermented into alcohol for use as motor fuel. Maybe one day we can forget about the oil from the Middle East and concentrate on old newspapers to run our cars.

Gene-spliced bacteria may solve another environmental crisis. Oil spills kill birds, sea mammals, and fish. They ruin beaches and destroy green plants that marine life needs for food. Cleaning up oil spills is expensive and difficult, but a tiny microbe may solve the problem. Dr. Ananda M. Chakrabarty, a scientist at the General Electric Research and Development Center in Schenectady, New York, has created a "hydrocarbon hungry microbe" that carries a piece of information on four plasmids donated by four different microbes, each of which had its own ability to consume petroleum. This new microbe can "eat" its way through crude oil many times faster than can any one of the single organisms it was made from.

Microbes are also being spliced together for mining. It is an expensive procedure to go through the leftovers of mining, called the tailings, to find minute particles of ore. These metal-hungry

A man-made microbe designed to attack oil spills on waterways, digesting the petroleum and converting it into a form that can be eaten by marine life, has been created in the laboratory by Dr. Ananda M. Chakrabarty, a scientist at the General Electric Research and Development Center. (General Electric Research and Devlopment Center)

microbes, each having a natural ability to digest one metal, together can separate platinum or gold from ore or from sea water. Other bacteria have been found that can withstand high concentrations of poisonous mercury, and one day they may be useful in cleaning up areas contaminated by that metal.

The wine industry is interested in engineered yeast that will ferment grapes faster and with better flavor. Food processors are eagerly waiting for the time when soybeans, which in some forms are difficult to digest, can be predigested by bacteria and made into soy milk and yogurt.

Bio-engineers are working on ways to make a special nitrogen-fixing bacteria that could be combined with plants that do not now have the ability to use the nitrogen in the air. Only legumes—peas, beans, alfalfa, and clover crops—now have such bacteria living on nodules on their roots. The bacteria fix the nitrogen from the air and make it into a form usable by the plant without the addition of fertilizer to the soil.

The possibilities of better things for a better life from re-combinant research seem endless. Vaccines will be developed, drugs will be mass-produced, there will be better food for more people, and even the process of aging may be changed.

Most scientists believe that only a small percentage of mi-crobes has been identified. We know of about 2,500. The more microbes found, the more tools scientists will have to work with for gene research.

Speculating on the kinds of things that may be possible by the end of the twentieth century, one scientist joked about making "little green men"—people who have chlorophyll to make their own food as plants do. It isn't always easy to sift the fact from the fiction, the jokes from the possible, the good from the bad direc-tons that biology should take. Not even the scientists agree. But the more the public understands, the more intelligently it can act on decisions that may be put to a vote.

8
Test-Tube Babies

BABY OF THE CENTURY . . . LITTLE MISS PERFECT . . . OUR MIRACLE
. . . banner headlines blazed on every newspaper. Every television
and radio newscast opened with the birth of Louise Joy Brown. This
5-pound 12-ounce infant girl was born at 11:47 P.M. on July 25,
1978, in a small hospital in the town of Oldham in northwestern
England. She was a normal, screaming baby, greeted by abnormal
screaming arguments of international interest.

Louise Brown was the world's first test-tube baby, and few
events in history have created so much controversy, called out so
many opinions. Hailed by some as a biological breakthrough and
condemned by others as a way for man to control and manipulate
life, the test-tube-baby issue will not be settled for a long time.

It has been the theme of sermons, the butt of comedians' jokes,
the subject of cartoons, and the backyard conversation of women
who consider it harmful or helpful.

Clergymen everywhere dwelt on the theme that life had been
created in a test tube.

It had not.

There are many things science and technology can help men

do, but, so far, creating life is not one of them. What, then, is the test-tube baby?

Some people imagine that test-tube babies grow in glass jars, as in *Brave New World*, in which babies grow on assembly lines and are "decanted" from bottles. That is as far from the truth as the story about the stork.

"*In vitro* fertilization," abbreviated IVF, is the name given to the technique. It simply means that the fertilization of the egg takes place in a glass dish instead of in the mother. It is not genetic engineering, not cloning (although it is one step in cloning), but only a way of helping, the way giving insulin or transplanting a kidney helps. Life is not created. It is only assisted. The technique is a detour in the usual system of development.

In order for a baby to be born, the same process has been necessary since the beginning of humanity. Every month an egg, a tiny cell not even as big as the dot of an *i*, is released from an ovary of the female on a signal sent by hormones. The ripe egg leaves the ovary and moves into the Fallopian tube. If sperm are present in the tube, the egg runs into them. A single sperm penetrates the outer membrane of the egg, and immediately a barrier is put up by the egg. No other sperm can enter.

The sperm has twenty-three chromosomes. The egg has twenty-three chromosomes. When they unite, when fertilization takes place, they produce a single cell of forty-six chromosomes, a full set of genetic information to make a human being. Immediately, the cell begins to divide into 2 cells, 4, 8, until it becomes what scientists call a blastocyst, a hollow ball-shaped cluster of about 100 cells. By this time, the egg has moved into the uterus and embedded itself in the uterus wall, where it will be nourished and grow for nine months.

At times there is a breakdown in the normal system. For one reason or another the sperm cannot reach the egg. Mrs. John Brown, the test-tube baby's mother, had such a problem. Her Fallopian tubes had become diseased and been surgically removed and the egg had no way to get from the ovary to meet the sperm.

The Browns had been waiting two years to adopt a child when they went to see Dr. Patrick Steptoe, a gynecologist at Oldham Hospital. With Dr. Robert Edwards, a physiologist at Cambridge University, Dr. Steptoe had been working for twelve years on developing a way to detour blocked Fallopian tubes. They had been successful with rabbits and monkeys and knew it was a procedure safe enough to try on a human.

The detour involved taking the egg from the mother's body, putting it into a glass dish where it would be fertilized with the father's sperm, and putting it back into the mother who would carry it for nine months.

The process sounds easy, but there are dozens of possibilities for failure at every step. Mrs. Brown was treated with hormones which sent signals to her ovaries to release a ripened egg. When he knew the egg was leaving the ovary, Dr. Steptoe made a tiny incision in Mrs. Brown's abdominal wall and inserted a laparoscope. The laparoscope is a long, thin instrument with an eyepiece and internal lighting, used to explore the abdomen without major surgery.

When he found the egg, Dr. Steptoe carefully removed it with a suction needle, transferring it immediately to a sterilized glass dish—not a test tube. The dish contained a mixture of blood serum and other nutrients to keep the egg alive.

Sperm from Mr. Brown was put into the dish with the egg. As soon as one of the sperm entered the egg, the fertilized egg was moved to another sterile dish with nutrients. No human baby had ever been seen growing from the absolute beginning, and no baby was ever watched over more attentively.

The egg began to divide. In two and a half days, when it had grown to eight cells, the decision to implant it in the mother was made. Although the cell can survive for many more divisions before it must be embedded in the uterus, the doctors had been most successful with an embryo younger than the blastocyst stage.

This step did not require microsurgery. Dr. Steptoe took a suction needle, lifted the egg from its dish, and placed it in Mrs. Brown's uterus. During this time, while her baby was beginning in the glass dish, Mrs. Brown had received hormone treatments that would prepare the lining of her uterus to receive the embryo. When the egg was replaced, everyone waited anxiously for nine months to go by.

To repeat, life had not been created—it had been assisted. People are worried for a variety of reasons. In the natural process of development, many embryos are miscarried or abort naturally. This seems to be nature's way of trying to select only normal, healthy babies to live and defective babies to be rejected.

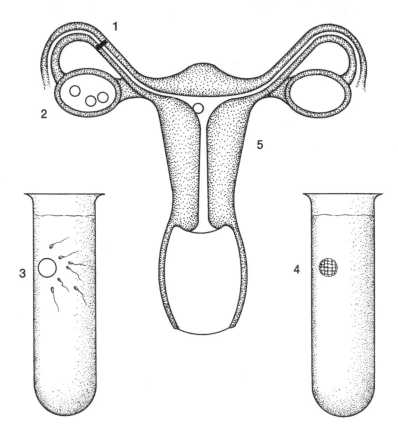

In vitro fertilization

1. Sometimes a Fallopian tube is blocked, and the egg cannot pass through it to meet a sperm.
2. The egg can be removed from the ovary with a suction needle.
3. It is placed in a test tube or glass dish, where it can be fertilized by a sperm from the father.
4. The egg begins to divide. When it has reached the blastula stage, a hollow ball of less than 100 cells, it is put back into the uterus of the mother.
5. Here it will embed itself in the uterine wall and develop for nine months.

People are afraid of the increased chance of defective babies being born with the test-tube-baby techniques. The chances are great that damage can be done at any stage from the taking of the egg to the replacement in the uterus. The egg is tiny, delicate, alive, and we don't even know all the influences of its hidden environment that affect it. If a test-tube baby is born defective, who is responsible? The parents? The doctors? Will the government be expected to care for it? Would anyone have the right to destroy an obviously defective embryo? Who would make that decision?

Bio-ethics is a term heard more frequently since we have learned to manipulate some of the life processes. The ethics of the biologists are becoming subjects of open forums and law courts.

One report says that 60 percent of fetuses do not make it out of the womb alive normally. Many eggs that are fertilized never even live long enough to become embedded in the uterus. What will happen to the race of man if the test-tube technique keeps defective fetuses alive? What if they grow up and have children and pass along defective genes?

During fertilization only the strongest, healthiest, most vigorous sperm reaches the egg and fertilizes it. This is one of nature's ways of insuring that the strong survive. In a glass dish, with all the sperm using the same nutrients, with the best of conditions, will each sperm have an equal chance of fertilizing the egg, or will there be a greater chance for a defective gene to be passed on?

Real battles, verbal and sometimes physical, rage over the abortion problem now. No one can decide to everyone's satisfaction at what moment a fertilized egg becomes a human being. Is it at the moment of fertilization, the moment it begins to divide and grow? If so, should the fertilized egg in a dish be considered a human with the right to life, or is it a bit of nonhuman matter that can be discarded if it appears to be abnormal?

Other objections come from people who fear that some women will "rent" their wombs—that is, carry a fertilized egg from another woman for nine months. There are laws governing artificial insemination, which is common, but none to guide people through the unknowns of *in vitro* fertilization. A woman "renting" her womb, carrying a child for another woman, would certainly contribute a great deal to that child. As her body nourished the fetus, everything she ate or drank or smoked would affect the child. Her emotional condition would have influence on the unborn infant.

Thousands of babies are born because artificial insemination has solved one problem, that of sterility in a man who would like to be a father. Sperm from a healthy male, sperm stored frozen in sperm banks, can be placed into a woman's uterus. From that point, it is entirely a natural process. The healthiest, most active sperm reaches the egg and fertilizes it. Natural selection takes place. A sperm damaged in the storage or transfer process would not be strong enough to fertilize the egg. For *in vitro* fertilization there is no such safeguard.

In 1932, when Huxley wrote *Brave New World*, his idea of a factory assembly line of babies in bottles, cared for by bottlers and decanters in the Central London Hatchery and Conditioning Centre, was not taken seriously. But when the headlines reported the first test-tube baby, people were afraid this fiction had come true.

It is unlikely we will come to factory-made babies. With the efficient, time-tested, low-cost method of producing babies now, why would we ever went to go to the expense or incur all the problems of a factory-made child?

The test-tube baby brought fears and questions, but it has also brought hope and good changes. For thousands of couples longing to have babies of their own, the *in vitro* technique seems like a miracle. Dr. Steptoe has announced the opening of clinics in Cambridge, England, and Norfolk, Virginia, to help couples with the problems Mr. and Mrs. Brown had.

In addition to being an answer to infertility, *in vitro* fertilization can help research on contraception. The world is greatly over-populated and people need information about how *not* to have babies, too.

In vitro fertilization's greatest help, however, will be as a technique for learning about birth defects. Doctors will be able to see when they happen and perhaps learn why they happen.

Test-tube babies will not be common because they are expensive and entail certain risks. Even Dr. Edwards told reporters, "We are in the early stages and still have a lot to learn."

But we do know how, and the techniques used in making test-tube babies are those necessary for some of the steps for cloning. What's next for this brave new world of biology?

9 *Send in the Clones*

When the imaginary Robert Wayne in Chapter One needed a kidney transplant, he called upon his clone for the necessary organs. He had been conditioned to accept the donation of a clone because it was commonly done in his society of the future. But Mr. Wayne, for all his conditioning, could not help wondering how the clone felt about his job.

How would you feel? Imagine yourself a fifteen-year-old clone assigned to the spare-parts farm where you would be on call for transplants of a leg, a kidney, or even your brain. Would you be angry? Terrified? Can you imagine how you might plot an escape, or do you think a society of clones would be brainwashed to accept this unpleasant role?

What would be the feelings of the cloned child of a famous violinist, with no ability to play a violin but talented as an auto mechanic? How would you assert your own personality, your freedom of choice?

How would you face life as one of a hundred look-alikes manning a space craft, a clone designed for special skills, size, or dexterity?

In our culture, we put great value on the opportunity to be

oneself, to do one's own thing, to be an individualist. The idea of a population of clones is frightening as well as fascinating.

Fortunately, we can focus on the fascinating and we need not be frightened. No mammal has yet been cloned directly from adult body cells, and we are a long way from the cloning of a human. But it is from this distance of time that we should consider the possibilities and outcomes of cell biology, that we should begin to understand the directions it can take. We should also understand the reasons for the research that has brought us this far in bio-engineering.

A clone is a carbon copy. A clone has the genetic information of only one parent. There is no mixing of genes with the chance for change. The word clone comes from *klon*, the Greek word meaning twig.

In some species, single parents produce offspring naturally, but these offspring are not clones. The process is called parthenogenesis, which comes from Greek and means virgin birth, the development of an unfertilized egg. (The virgin goddess, Athena, was honored in a temple in Athens called the Parthenon, meaning the place of the virgin.) Many lower forms of animals can begin to develop without fertilization. In one series of experiments, a researcher was able to produce sea urchins from one parent in 371 different ways, including shaking, heating, and treating them with chemicals. An animal born by parthenogenesis is not a clone because it will have only half the usual number of chromosomes, only those from the egg, while a clone has a full set of chromosomes.

Another process common in nature and interesting to cell biologists is called regeneration. It is the ability to grow new parts. If someone grabs a lizard, such as the little chameleon, he is likely to be left with only a tail in his hand while the animal scurries away. The lizard can twist off its tail and grow a new one, not quite as long or graceful as the old one, but still a tail.

A tiny flatworm called planaria has been the subject of many experiments. Its head is sliced into four parts and it grows four new heads, or its tail is cut in two and it grows two tails. It regenerates. We, too, regenerate some parts, not arms or legs, but new liver cells, new skin cells, red blood cells. The cells, in regeneration, get a signal to start growing again, even though they had stopped creating that part. That is what interests the biologists. What signals do the cells get? How do they get them?

Both regeneration and parthenogenesis are providing clues to the ways in which cells get the signals to grow and develop. In most cellular research, the goal is not cloning, but using the techniques of cloning to discover how the cell works.

Science-fiction movies, television, and books have filled our minds with fantasies of cloning armies full of Hitlers, stages full of Mozarts, space ships manned by specially made workers. We tend to forget that cloning is an ancient art and that it can provide advantages other than duplicating people.

Cloning a plant is quite simple. Anyone who has ever taken a leaf from an African violet and put it in water to grow has done it. It is growing a plant that will have genes identical with those of its parent. No seed was used, there was no fertilization, no male and female took part.

In many biology classes, cloning a carrot is a standard lab experiment. In the early 1960s, at the Laboratory for Cell Physiology at Cornell University, Dr. Frederick C. Steward cloned a carrot for the first time. This was not just growing a carrot from the cut-off top in a dish on the windowsill. He took a cell from the body of the carrot, a cell already differentiated, a cell that had followed the directions for making its different parts, such as root, stem, leaf. This cell contained all the DNA, all the genetic information to make a carrot, and Dr. Steward stimulated the nucleus of that cell so that it began to divide and grow.

In cloning a carrot in the classroom, a culture of aseptic cells, cells free from contamination, is established. The secret is the use of sterile laboratory technique. After tiny sections of a carrot seedling are cut with a sterile razor blade or scalpel, they are put on a nutrient medium in a petri dish. This medium is made up of agar (a gelatin-like substance) to support the tissue, organic and inorganic salts, vitamins, amino acids, coconut milk, and some auxins (hormones for plant growth). Clumps of cells called the callus tissue will grow from the cut stem sections. This callus is a mass of undifferentiated cells, cells that have not yet begun to be parts of the plant. Each cell will grow into a carrot and each carrot will be genetically like the original. They are clones.

Cloning of an animal is much more complicated. Plants are known as "totipotent," which means that each cell can express its complete genetic plan. Animals must grow from an egg.

A frog has twenty-six chromosomes. The egg has thirteen and

the sperm has thirteen. When they join in fertilization the number is again twenty-six. In the 1950s, at the Institute for Cancer Research in Philadelphia, Robert Briggs and Thomas King pioneered a method of cloning using the nuclear-transplant method. They used frogs because the eggs are large and fairly easy to work with. They took a frog egg and destroyed the nucleus. Then they took a cell from a frog embryo, a body cell with the full set of chromosomes, and took out its nucleus. They put the nucleus from the frog embryo into that egg. The nucleus from the donor gives the instructions for development.

When they tried this nuclear transplant with cells from adult frogs, they were not successful and they thought that this was because the older cells had differentiated too much.

Later, in the 1960s, John B. Gurdon, a British biologist, made real progress when he cloned healthy adult African clawed frogs. Instead of taking cells from embryo frogs, he took cells from the intestines of young tadpoles, cells that had already differentiated. In 1975, Gurdon's group cloned tadpoles from the skin cells of adult frogs. They proved that the genes of completely differentiated cells could be made to develop even after they had the message to "turn off."

The hardest part of this work is getting the growth of the egg to synchronize with the growth of the new nucleus. Egg cells divide faster than body cells, and if cells are not dividing at the same rate, the chromosomes break and either the clone will not develop or it will be deformed.

How a frog is cloned

1. The nucleus is removed from a frog egg. It is now called an enucleated egg.
2. A section of intestine is taken from a tadpole (a young frog).
3. A cell from that intestinal tissue is taken and its nucleus removed.
4. The nucleus (with all its hereditary instructions) from the tadpole cell is put into the enucleated frog egg.
5. The egg, with its new nucleus, begins to divide and develop into a tadpole and then an adult frog. The frog's genes are exactly like those of the tadpole because its instructions came only from the nucleus of the tadpole. The frog is a clone.

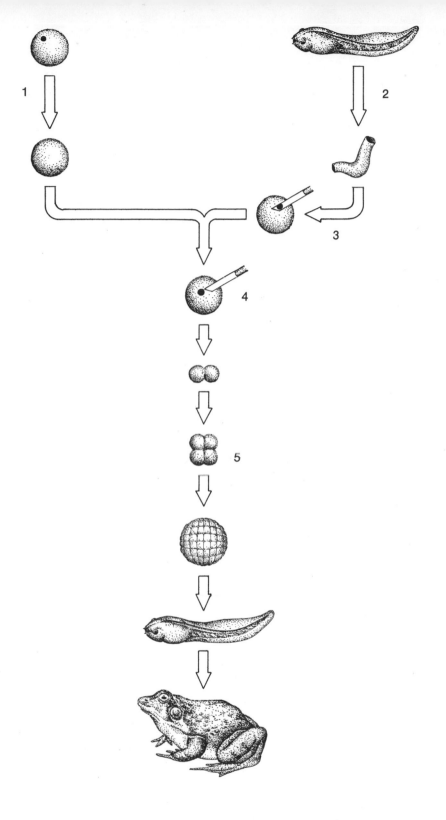

Gurdon figured out a way to get better synchronization by using a "serial transfer," two or more nuclear transfers. In the first step the nucleus from the cell of the animal to be cloned is put into an egg that had its nucleus destroyed. The embryo begins to grow. At a very early stage, when the embryo is still a ball of cells and the cells have not yet received their signals to differentiate, the cells are separated and the nuclei from those cells are transplanted into another set of eggs. It is from this second set of eggs that the clones grow. It is a bit more complicated, but it works better because the cells from that second set of transplants are dividing at a rate more nearly like the rate of growth of the egg cell. Using this serial transfer, Gurdon successfully cloned adult African clawed frogs that could reproduce.

Cloning mammals is much more difficult than cloning frogs. Frogs' eggs are ten to twenty times larger than mammalian eggs, and frogs can grow in a tank of water. Mammals must be nurtured in the womb of animals.

Improved instruments for microsurgery have made it possible to work with mammalian eggs. Nuclei from mouse and rabbit cells have been emplanted into mouse and rabbit eggs.

Parthenogenesis can be promoted in mouse eggs by stimulating the egg, usually with a pin prick or a chemical. Clement Markert at Yale University had done this, and he began to wonder about the part the sperm played in the development of the embryo. He wondered whether the sperm, along with adding half the number of chromosomes, added some substance or stimulation to get things started.

Markert put mouse spern into an egg, and then, microsurgically, he took out the sperm nucleus (called the pronucleus) before it had a chance to add its half number of chromosomes to the egg's pronucleus. But the results were no better than before. Maybe, he thought, this was because there were only half the number of chromosomes left. Something was missing.

Another biology laboratory had found a substance called Cytochalasin B made from fungus. It inhibits cell division but it does not seem to interfere with the replication of chromosomes in the nucleus. By adding this, Markert got the egg to double its number of chromosomes and to grow. He did not get adult mice, but soon two other biologists did. Seven single-parent mice were born alive at the Jackson Laboratory in Bar Harbor, Maine.

The mice had the same genetic pattern as their mother; they had inherited her half of the chromosomes, which were then doubled. They were semi-clones.

If those semi-clones are used as donors, the offspring would be clones, exact duplicates. Only the female animal can be produced by this method, even if the sperm nucleus were used instead of the egg nucleus. If an egg, which has an X chromosome, is duplicated by the chemical, it will have a normal XX set. If the sperm nucleus, with its X or Y chromosomes, is duplicated, the result will be either an XX, or female, or a YY, which could not survive. A male clone can be made only from the transfer of a nucleus from a body cell. The sex of the clone will always be the same as that of the donor.

One of the many good reasons for not attempting human cloning is the fact that humans cannot be treated like laboratory animals. A woman would have to agree to donate her egg. By the same techniques used to produce the test-tube baby, the egg would have to be removed surgically after it left the ovary. Its nucleus would be destroyed and the nucleus from a body cell of the donor put in. The egg, stimulated to grow from the new nucleus, would be put back into the woman carrier's uterus. Many things can go wrong.

The possibility of deformity is much greater in a cloned embryo than in a test-tube baby. If the embryo is deformed, can it be discarded? Is it a person, with all the rights of a human being?

Even if we could copy a human, which we cannot do now, we could never produce a clone the same age as the donor. There must be a time gap. The donor must be older than its clone, and the two can never have the advantages of the same environment of growth that identical twins have.

Identical twins come from the same egg, the same mother, and are born at the same time under the same conditions. A clone is born at a different time from the donor, from another egg, into another environment. Much of what we are and do is influenced by our environment. Genius, talent, achievement, greatness are the results of time and place as well as of inheritance. Being in the right place at the right time or being exposed to certain sets of circumstances can alter a personality, stifle or encourage creativity. One scientist said, "The clone of Hitler might be a nice guy, a good neighbor, and the clone of Einstein could be bright but have no aptitude for math at all."

A clone could be a very lonely person, have tremendous mental pressures because of his lack of relationships. People have family bonds, a set of parents, a status in the community. Would a clone? If the day ever comes when clones of humans are made, the law courts will be backlogged with cases involving the rights of clones and clone owners.

Joshua Lederberg, now head of the Rockefeller University, has said, "Nobody has given me any reason why I'd want to spend a nickel to clone human beings." But some people argue otherwise.

What reasons for cloning a person could justify the risks, the ethical and legal fights?

If nuclear warfare is ever used on a massive scale, millions will be killed, but even greater numbers might be left sterile from radiation or genetically damaged. Then there might be a reason to use the healthy, genetically undamaged humans as donors for cloning. Some people might want to clone a dying child, or to clone identical people for research. Others might see cloning as a way of providing a child to an infertile couple.

It might be possible to develop the cloning technique to grow replacement parts rather than entire bodies. A heart or kidney clone, developed in a laboratory, would be insurance for a longer life.

The general agreement among sensible scientists right now seems to be that the ability to clone a human is not sufficient reason to do so. Medicine is not an industry, and people are not products.

Why continue the research on cloning, then?

Right now cloning is a technique for learning more about the cell. We still need to know how the cell differentiates, how it turns on and off to the messages. The techniques of cloning teach us about the runaway cells of cancer that do not seem to remember how to turn off. They can tell us about aging and immunology, and they can be useful in designing chemicals to control the differentiation of cells.

Cloning will continue to be the subject of novels and movies, the arguments of ministers and lawyers. Instead of fantasizing about human clones taking over the job market, we should consider the exciting ways in which cloning is working for us now.

10 Cloned Forests, Farms, and Zoos

A whole forest can be shipped by air in two small boxes. An acre of flowers can be grown on the shelves of one room. A herd of cattle can be transported inside a group of rabbits. All these things are the result of cloning or techniques learned from cloning. This kind of cloning is going to be used more and more in order to feed, clothe, and house the growing world population. Cloning has moved from the laboratory to the production line of agriculture and horticulture.

The ancient art of cloning plants—grafting, slipping, using cuttings—has become the science of tissue culture. Florists are happy with the results because it provides flowers faster, better, and cheaper.

When a nurseryman plants a field of daisies, he takes chances. He hopes that the weather will be good, that there will not be a sudden freeze which will kill the seedlings. He may plant a pure strain of seeds, but he is taking a chance with genetics, of getting a mixture of tall and short plants, different shapes of flowers, and different mixtures of color. He would need a half-acre of land to grow 1,000 plants. If he uses tissue culture, he can raise 1,000 daisies on 30 feet of shelf space, and from one cutting he can grow a million plants in a year.

Gerbera daisies take from seven to nine months to grow from seedling to bloom when raised in the usual way, but only ninety days when grown in a test tube. The grower will also know that the crop of daisies will be the exact color, shape, and size of the daisy from which he takes the original cell. Flowers from seed are the result of genetic pairing, with the chances for change. Flowers from a cell are as predictable as if they came from a machine. It is better business, but it does, of course, take away some of nature's nice surprises.

When tourists drive across the Peace Bridge from the United States into Canada, the customs inspector asks if they have any plants in their car. Live plants are not allowed to be taken across international borders. Each country tries to keep plant diseases, parasites, and damaging insects from spreading to its crops. Shipping cloned plants eliminates that problem because the cloned plants are "clean." They carry no disease because they have been raised in sterile conditions.

Cloned plant cells can be quick-frozen in liquid nitrogen and kept indefinitely in storage for use any time.

Tissue culture brings a change in the kinds of jobs for people in agriculture. A nurseryman generally hires men and women to work in greenhouses and fields. Now he hires a plant pathologist or microbiologist to organize a laboratory, and a staff of technicians to wash and sterilize equipment, make the medium, attend to the cuttings and transfers.

Farmers are seeing the good results of cloning. In Taiwan, they are raising potatoes and pineapples from cells—a marvelous advantage for countries with limited cropland. In the United States, they are experimenting with asparagus, which is expensive in markets, especially when the buyer is fussy about getting all stalks the same size. Cloned asparagus is cheaper and more attractive to the buyer.

Cloned wheat that is rust-resistant is being produced. Farmers have always cross-bred crops in an effort to grow disease-free plants with the highest yield possible, but cloners, starting with a single cell from a stalk of wheat or other grain they know has produced a perfect grain, can get predictable results. They do not have to gamble on the hereditary shuffle.

Tree farmers are using the tissue-culture techniques to great advantage, too. According to federal reports, 22 percent of Ameri-

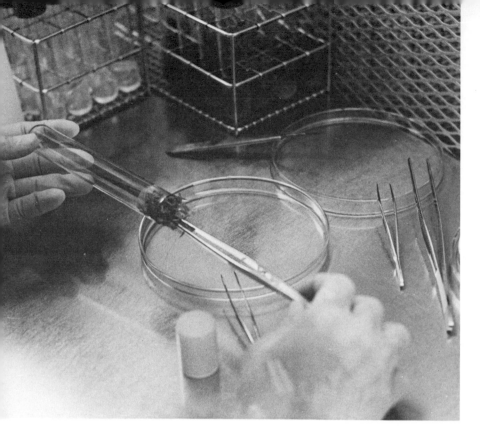

Some clusters are put back into fresh test tubes for reculture. The largest part of the crop is put in the rooting container to be sold to wholesale growers, and some are sold separately as "test-tube babies" to the retail market. (Oglesby Nursery, Inc.)

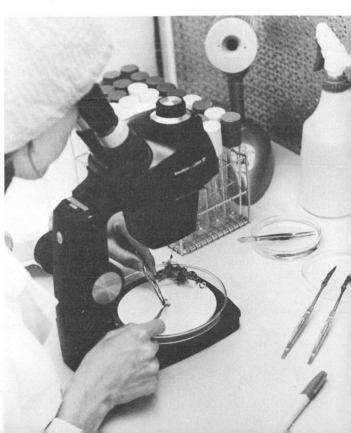

A technician must use a microscope to cut the first tissue from the donating plant. (Oglesby Nursery, Inc.)

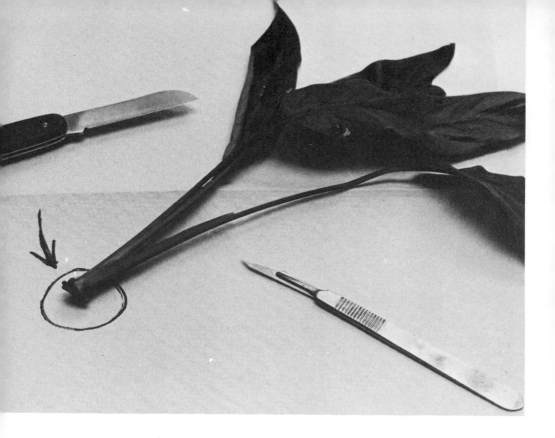

This is the source, the
original plant from
which the cells are taken
to grow thousands of
plants just like it. It
is called the explant.
(Oglesby Nursery, Inc.)

A commercial "test-tube
baby" produced by a nur-
sery makes it a simple
matter to ship plants and
grow them under controlled
conditions. (Oglesby
Nursery, Inc.)

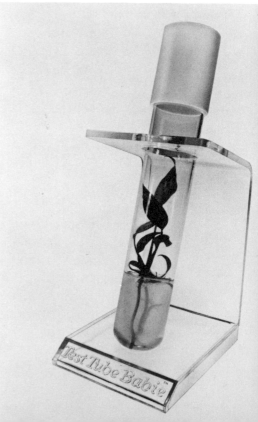

ca's lands are used for commercial forests, compared to 19 percent for cropland. The forest area is owned by the government, individual farmers, and great lumber corporations, and together they are raising more trees than they were thirty years ago. The higher production is a direct result of forestry science, of trained people managing trees as a crop, cutting and replanting them in a regular cycle. Their techniques have also developed stronger trees, resistant to disease, parasites, and insect damage. But with cloning, tree farming has been given an additional boost by using test-tube babies for the woods.

A Canadian lumber company reported that with 1 gallon of nutrient medium they can grow 3 million white spruce plantlets from single cells. Whole forests of genetically selected trees can be guaranteed. No longer will a lumberman have to go through a forest grading trees, selecting those that will be cut. Because all the seedlings planted will be exactly the same, lumbermen can cut a whole stand of trees at once. As soon as an area is cleared of trees, it is replanted with seedlings.

Plant cloning is a reality. It has taken the long step from research to production. Animal cloning is still in the research stage, but all reports point to ways in which it too will become a useful tool.

Millions of animals are raised for research. There are commercial firms whose business is supplying mice, rats, monkeys, rabbits, dogs, and other animals for this purpose. The important requirement for a laboratory animal is knowledge of its strain, its genetic background. In order for a mouse, for example, to be a valuable research "tool" for cancer, the researcher must know whether the mouse's parents had cancer, tumors, or diseases of any kind. It takes five years of breeding, of selecting the right parents, to produce a pure strain of mice. Decades could be needed to produce by selective breeding a prize bull or a prize race horse.

When cloning techniques are perfected for mammals, it will be possible to take a body cell from a prize race horse and clone as many copies as there are brood mares to carry the foals. One scientist points out, however, that we may run into what he calls "the Spanish-galleon effect." If a Spanish galleon loaded with rare coins was found on the bottom of the ocean, the coins soon would have little value because there would be so many of them exactly alike.

Would prize horses, cattle, and dogs lose their value with lots of copies?

Like the shipping of forests and fields of flowers across international borders, it is also possible to ship herds of cattle. These are not cloned cattle, but "test-tube-baby" cattle, created by using some of the techniques of cloning.

If, in Africa for example, there is a need for a kind of cattle that produces a lot of milk and also is resistant to specific diseases, a kind of cattle that happens to live in the United States, those cattle cannot be shipped to Africa. Federal laws regulate transportation of animals in order to prevent the spread of disease.

But a herd of cattle can be shipped before the cattle are born, before they have to comply with regulations or have been exposed to disease. First, a prize cow is selected, for her high milk yield or her special resistance to disease. She is treated with hormones so that she superovulates—that is, her ovaries release many ripe eggs at one time. The eggs are flushed from her body in a process which is painless and requires no surgery. In a sterile dish in a lab, the eggs are fertilized with sperm from a prize bull, the same method that is used for a test-tube baby. When the fertilized eggs have begun to divide and are on their way to healthy development, each egg is put into the uterus of a rabbit.

The rabbits have been receiving hormones to prepare the uterine walls to accept the embryos. The beginning cow embryo, now only a few cells in size, embeds itself in a rabbit uterus and doesn't seem to know whether its new home is owned by a cow or a rabbit. It begins to grow. The embryo can live as long as eight days in the rabbit, long enough to ship the rabbit by air to another country. At the destination, the embryos are removed from the rabbits and transplanted into native cows where they develop and are born.

Dr. T. C. Hsu at the M.D. Anderson Tumor Institute in Houston, Texas, has so much faith in the future of cloning that he has a "clone zoo," a collection of more than 200 potential sources of wild animals. Dr. Hsu and his staff are studying cells and they need a wide variety of cells from as many different kinds of animals as they can find. He has asked zoologists all over the world to supply him with a snip of skin from whatever animal they are studying. His clone zoo collection is a commendable sideline of his major research.

Snipping a bit of skin from a tiger, a white rhinoceros, a rare bird, or small mammal does not injure the animal, and the wound heals quickly. Dr. Hsu said, "The fur grows over it and the animal is none the worse for donating cells for the future."

The cells are frozen quickly with liquid nitrogen at −196 degrees Celsius. "We may lose 20 percent of the cells," said Dr. Hsu,

Cow embryo shipped in rabbit uterus

1. Eggs are taken from a cow.
2. They are fertilized in a laboratory dish and begin to grow in the nutrient solution.
3. When they have reached the hollow ball or blastula stage, each embryo is placed in a rabbit uterus.
4. The rabbit is shipped to another country . . .
5. . . . and the embryo taken from the rabbit and replaced in the uterus of a cow.

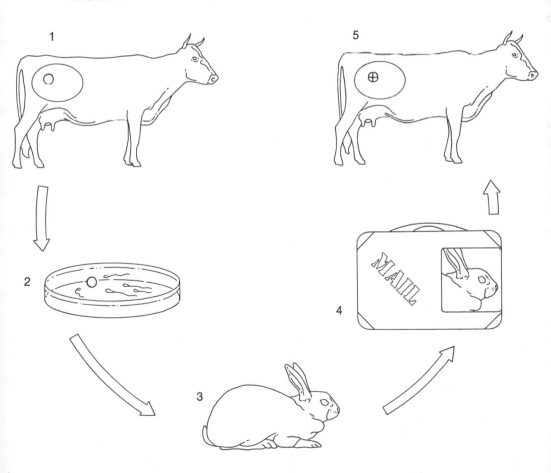

"but in an ampule of 10 million cells from one animal, our recovery rate is good."

These cells will last forever. Two thousand years from now they can be thawed and white rhinos or snow leopards or gorillas can be cloned from them. It is not science fiction.

Once in a while a newspaper reports the finding of a frozen woolly mammoth in the ice fields of Siberia. One such article speculated on the possibility of taking cells from a frozen mammoth and cloning them, using elephants as the carrying females. Dr. Hsu does not believe this would be possible, because the tissue is dead. "You must start with living cells."

That should put to rest the half-joking suggestions that the mummy of King Tut could be cloned or the revival of other historical figures brought about. It can't be done. But with a combination of recombinant DNA and cloning techniques, we will be able to produce cobless corn with the seeds on the tassel, a technique being researched now by DeKalb Ag-Research Inc. We will find out how to produce low-fat milk with "built in" vitamin D in extra amounts, new kinds of meat with lower fat, better flavor, and less susceptibility to spoilage. We will have new flavors in fish and fowl. One lab is working on a naked chicken—a mutant strain of chickens that don't grow feathers but put more energy into meat growth.

Maybe someday, if we conserve our wild lands, we can restock them with the wild animals that are becoming extinct. Maybe we can save the elephant, the gorilla, the tiger.

Cell biology has come a long way from Leeuwenhoek's "wee beasties."

11 *Back to Spontaneous Generation*

We have come a long way, but we are circling back to an old question that Louis Pasteur thought he had put to rest forever. Pasteur was a genius, a one-in-a-million kind of thinker, and he did not do things by halves. When he set out to disprove the idea that germs and lower forms of life spring from the air or from non-living matter, he planned a series of dramatic experiments. As part of the demonstration he collected air in sterile flasks, air from the courtyard of the Paris Observatory, from a balloon 2,700 feet over country fields, and from the sparkling ice fields of the Alps where he carried his equipment 6,500 feet up Mont Blanc.

On April 7, 1864, at a scientific meeting at the Sorbonne in Paris, Pasteur triumphantly announced, "Never will the doctrine of spontaneous generation recover from the mortal blow that this simple experiment has dealt it." And he finished with the statement, "There is now no circumstance known in which it can be affirmed that microscopic beings come into the world without germs, without parents similar to themselves."

He was right. Given the circumstances of the earth today, with its atmosphere, its surface water, and the temperature of the planet, life must come from existing life.

But where did it come from originally? It must have started once. How? Scientists are again thinking about spontaneous generation.

There are several theories. Anyone can choose which to believe because there is no proof. No one was there.

First, there is the theory that life has always been here, that it did not have a beginning. It is hard to make an argument for this one because everything in nature points to a beginning and an end.

Another theory assumes a creator. All religions throughout history have believed in such a master planner. Those who interpret the Bible as fact believe that the earth was created in six days, with all the life on it. Others believe in a creator whose creation followed a slow plan rather than a "zap," instant kind of beginning. Evolution and religion can go together.

A third theory suggests that life came from outer space, another universe. There is no proof that life exists anywhere except on earth, but that does not mean it does not. We cannot rule out this theory, but it evades the question. Where did the life from outer space come from? It had to have a beginning.

Then we come to the theory of biogenesis, the idea Pasteur proved, that life always comes from life. It does. Spontaneous generation does not work on this planet under conditions today. But 5 billion years ago, when this planet was, according to Genesis, "without form, and void," life as we know it could not happen. For millions and millions of years the earth was a hot, molten, burning mass, and when it cooled it was barren. The water vapor suspended in the atmosphere began to condense and the eons of rain began, the time of oceans forming, washing over the earth's entire surface.

What was needed for life to begin? Warm temperature, water, atoms of carbon, hydrogen, nitrogen, oxygen, and phosphorus, a source of energy, and time. Time is the key. Endless eons of time in which all kinds of combinations happen by chance. There is a theory that if a chimpanzee was put at a typewriter and allowed to hit keys for twenty-five years, enough words would emerge by chance to make a novel. Enough time could allow chemical combinations to create life.

The elements were there—simple compounds of hydrogen, nitrogen, oxygen, and phosphorus dissolved in the oceans. The atmosphere was not like earth's today, which is a blanket around the earth. A layer of ozone in the upper atmosphere protects us from too much radiation from our energy source, the sun. The ancient atmosphere was probably made up of water vapor, hydrogen, ammonia, and methane. The sun beat down, creating a brilliantly colored sky as the colors were absorbed by the molecules of gases. The ultraviolet light from these unprotected rays of sun provided energy. Lightning provided energy, too, forcing the elements into many combinations. Some combinations lasted, others did not.

Hundreds of millions of years of changing combinations, by chance forming links of amino acids and nucleotides, created a great ocean of soup. Scientists call it the primordial soup, and it was probably thick with chemicals. It could not exist now and there is nothing like it on earth. Today it would be eaten up. It existed simply because there was no life to consume it.

A clue to how much soup would have been consumed is the fact that a bacteria can double in twenty minutes; that means there will be 8 in an hour, 64 in two hours, and 32,768 in five hours. Dr. Hoagland, explaining this rapid growth of bacteria, said, "If *E. coli* could continue to grow with plenty of food for twenty-four hours, the mass of cells would cover the earth a mile deep!"

When life did form in that primordial soup, it thrived, grew, and consumed all the food in the oceans. Nothing was left, so that early life had to change, evolve, adapt to other ways of getting food.

Scientists are so sure the soup could have existed that they have re-created it in the laboratory. In 1953, at the University of Chicago, chemist Stanley Miller put together the elements of the early atmosphere in a flask. He had water vapor, hydrogen, ammonia, and methane. He created a "miniature lightning," a 60,000-volt spark. The water vapor and gases drifted through the spark for a week. Liquid condensed, drop by drop, and gradually collected in another flask. Miller analyzed it and found four different kinds of amino acids and half a dozen other compounds, the beginning of the primordial soup. If that could emerge in a week, it is not hard to believe that all kinds of things could emerge in millions of years.

Other experiments proved that these links, the amino acids and nucleotides from the first tests, could be made to connect into DNA-like chains and protein-like chains. To make a cell, more millions of years of trial and error produced enzymes, and millions more years of reactions formed DNA that could replicate. Then

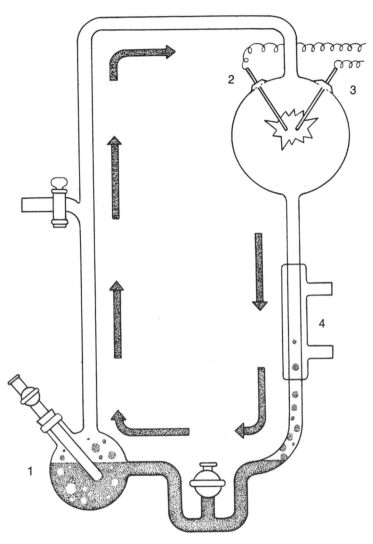

Diagram of the apparatus Miller used to duplicate conditions believed to have existed when life began on earth.

1. Boiling water changes into water vapor.
2. It mixes with the gases from the hypothetical primitive atmosphere—hydrogen, methane, and ammonia—
3. . . . passes through an electric spark . . .
4. . . . and then condenses, leaving water and organic compounds. He imitated the primitive conditions of heavy rains, moderate heat, lightning, and the chemicals of the atmosphere.

something had to develop to contain this, a membrane to hold the cell together.

Life did happen, and probably only once. In science it is usually the simple truth that prevails. The simple explanation fits the re-created evidence of the lab.

All living creatures, without exception, are made of the same materials—the four nucleotides, the twenty amino acids—and have the same system for conducting the business of living. If life had been created more than once, if it had started over with each class of animals, it seems likely that there would also be more than one kind of living machinery.

But we don't know. And probably we shall never have anything but theory.

12 *The Making of a Scientist*

> Those who have torches will pass them along.
>
> Plato, *The Republic*

SWEET-PEA PATCH GETS GOLDEN FLEECE AWARD. If Gregor Mendel were alive today, that might be a headline in one of our papers. It would not be surprising to read ARMADILLOS COST TAXPAYERS THOUSANDS, or perhaps SNAKES GET MILKED AS TAXPAYERS GET BILKED.

Are we being fooled by the scientists? Is the public being fleeced? Are we paying for labs full of armadillos, molds, mushrooms, and monkeys and getting no return for our investment? A senator in Washington, intent on pointing out waste in governmental spending, presents a tongue-in-cheek "Golden Fleece" award for the most ridiculous project funded by the government. Most of the time he does point the finger at awful waste, but sometimes the award makes people feel as though all studies are silly. It is easy to have a distorted impression of scientific research if we don't understand how it will work for us in the long run.

Armadillos, for example, are being used to find a cure for

leprosy. Bees, wasps, and snakes are "milked" to study the enzyme action of venom, which might be useful in cancer research. If Mendel had applied for a government grant to pay for his pea patch, he might have aroused the wrath of non-scientists who could not see beyond the peas to the real reason for the study.

Scientific research requires money. Scientists get money by writing requests for funds. Often writing the application for a grant, planning the project in detail, with budgets, staff, and equipment, is the major portion of the work itself.

There are two kinds of research—basic and applied.

Basic research is the exploration into the unknown, the search for new knowledge. There are no guidebooks, no manuals of procedure. The scientist is alone with his or her imagination and curiosity. No one says, "You must come up with a new concept by August 30." There is no time limit. The only limit, in fact, is that of the scientist's mind. Basic research is the real frontier, the search for something the searcher hopes will be there, but the readiness to find something quite different. Lewis Thomas, in his book called *The Lives of a Cell*, said that the ingredient that distinguishes applied from basic research is the element of surprise. And he also said that a good way to tell how the work is going in a research lab is to listen in the corridors. "If you hear the word, 'Impossible!' spoken as an expletive, followed by laughter, you will know that someone's orderly research plan is coming along nicely."

Applied research is technology. It is taking the facts, the results of basic research, and using them to create something useful for mankind. It is no less important or complex. The main difference is in the plan, the organization. And the workers hope there will be no surprises.

The elimination of polio as one of the dread diseases in the 1940s is a great example of a combination of basic and applied research working together.

Basic research isolated the virus that causes polio. Then with outstanding organization and planning, the labs went to work producing a vaccine. Without the basic research, scientists, engineers, and technicians would have had to develop more and better iron lungs, braces, hospitals, and therapy methods, but the disease would have kept on.

The flight to the moon was the result of years and years of basic research in physics and astronomy. Then the engineers took over and applied the knowledge to building equipment that allowed the men to eat, breathe, and generally survive in an alien environment. Once the principles of aerodynamics and energy were known, technologists found ways to build rockets and supply fuel.

Applied research does not take second place to basic research. One without the other is like a seed left unplanted.

Applied research gave us vital equipment like the kidney dialysis machine, techniques such as heart transplants, and surgical and chemical treatment for cancer. But only basic research, only *new* knowledge, will find a cure for cancer, heart disease, genetic disease, or kidney malfunction. Medical care in the United States costs about $150 billion a year. Only half of one percent of those billions is spent on basic research. This is not because the scientists are not trying to get backing for their investigations. Hundreds of scientists cannot find jobs because funding is cut, and for every scientist out of work there is a lag in the race for knowledge.

Not every scientist is a Nobel Prize winner, a Watson, Crick, or Avery. Not everyone who works on a project is a Ph.D. Research is a team effort. No one works alone. The support systems are vital. Only a few are chosen to walk on the moon or rendezvous in space, but hundreds of technicians, engineers, electricians, file clerks, and tool makers are part of the team, too.

Dr. Willard Elliott, a biochemist at the State University of New York at Buffalo, is an example of a team leader on a project paid for by public money, a project that might need explaining. Any warm summer day, Dr. Elliott, or a group of his graduate students, can be found bundled in white coveralls, beekeepers' face masks, and gloves, collecting bee and wasp nests. He even gets neighbors to help when he can find one curious enough to ask what he is doing up on a ladder against the eaves of a house.

Dr. Elliott holds out a plastic tray covered with a weak-voltage electric grid, and when the agitated bees or wasps land on it, they get a slight shock. That makes them react by stinging the tray. They release a substance called a pheromone, which signals others to join them. Back at the lab, the venom is collected and analyzed by technicians. Other assistants care for and milk the snakes kept in the lab for venom analysis. They also take care of equipment, keep records, type, and file. Dr. Elliott and his associates publish papers about their experimental results, sharing with other scientists the world over their information about specific enzyme action in venoms.

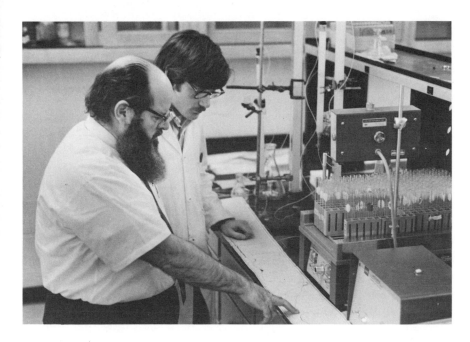

Dr. Willard B. Elliott and Dr. George W. Shepard discuss a gel permeation chromatogram of honey bee venom. It is the first step in purification of the venom. (State University of N.Y. at Buffalo)

For every team leader who is a Ph.D., there may be dozens of people skilled at things as various as using the electron microscope or glass blowing. Sometimes carpenters, electricians, and plumbers become part of the group as they devise equipment that will be used in the study. Science has come a long way from Robert Hooke devising his experiments for the weekly Royal Society meetings.

How does a person become a scientist? There is an old saying that the way to eat an elephant is one bite at a time. The way to become a scientist is one step at a time, beginning in high school by taking as much science and math as possible. Take biology, chemistry, physics, and in the summer apply for jobs at research institutes. Most hospitals have laboratories which can use unskilled help. Sweeping in a lab is at least a way of being exposed to what is going on there. Taking care of lab animals requires very little training, only a lot of common sense.

Do well enough in high school to get into college. It would be nice if everyone could go to a school like Princeton, Stanford, or

California Institute of Technology, but that isn't possible. However, another old saying, among parents especially, is that you get out of college what you put into it. Wherever you go to college—a small local school, a big state university, or a private college—you learn what you try to learn. It pays to do well in college, because the next step is the big one, the important one. Graduate school. A bachelor's degree is only part way to a research job. When a science student is ready for the long haul of graduate school, he or she looks around for a "mentor," a person who will be a guide through the doctoral program. For example, people go to Cal Tech for the privilege of studying under Linus Pauling. Students try for a teaching assistantship, known as a TA, which is about as low on the totem pole of teaching as possible, but pays the expenses of graduate school. Graduate students teach freshman lab courses or assist professors in some way while also taking courses. As in medical school or law school, they continue taking courses for three or four years, but unlike medical school a science degree requires some individual research. In order to earn a Ph.D., you must get into the great race, add a piece of new knowledge, look into something no one else has found before. That research might take a few years, and afterward it is necessary to write a dissertation, which is like writing a book about the research. The last step, often called the "orals," is to defend the thesis in front of a group of other scientists. They then decide whether to award that cherished and hard-won doctorate.

Does it sound like a lot of work? It is. Only those who really want to, who feel they must, should choose to do it.

If that is not for you, and of course it is not for most, there are dozens of careers related to science that do not require a Ph.D. You can be a botanist, horticulturist, medical librarian, scientific illustrator, medical secretary, chemist, X-ray technician, radiologist, glass blower, lab technician, bio-statistician—the field is very wide.

Exploration today may be ballooning across the Atlantic or challenging Mount Everest, but it can also be working with thousands of fruit flies, building wire models, or finding a way to transport a herd of cattle inside a colony of rabbits.

Remember Pasteur's words: "chance favors the prepared mind." Prepare your mind so when the chance comes for you to make a contribution, to get into the great adventure, to explore the unknown, you will be ready.

Glossary

AMINO ACID. The molecules that are the basic building blocks of proteins. There are about twenty amino acids.

ANIMALCULES. The name given to the tiny protozoa Leeuwenhoek saw under his microscopes.

ASTER. A star-shaped structure named by Flemming to describe the tangled arrangement of chromosomes during cell division. The term is now used to describe the pattern formed by tiny fibrils that radiate away from the centrioles during cell division.

ATOM. The smallest particle of an element that can take part in a chemical reaction.

BACTERIOPHAGE. A "bacteria-eating" virus that enters a bacterium and causes it to produce viruses.

BACTERIUM. A one-celled form of life that is smaller and simpler than plant or animal cells and does not have an organized nucleus.

BIOGENESIS. The theory that all living things are produced only from other living things.

BLASTULA. An early stage in the embryonic development of animals. It is a sphere of a single layer of cells surrounding a fluid-filled cavity.

CARBOHYDRATES. Molecules containing only carbon, hydrogen, and oxygen in which the ratio of hydrogen atoms to carbon atoms is two to one. They are the main nutrients that supply energy to animals. Examples are glucose, sucrose, and starches.

CENTRIFUGE. A machine that spins mixtures at high speeds, separating the substances by the differences in their densities. The more dense materials fall to the bottom and the less dense remain at the top.

CHROMOSOMES. Structures in the nucleus of a cell composed of DNA and protein and containing all the genetic information of the cell.

DIABETES. A disease characterized by a high sugar level in the blood, caused by the lack of insulin from the pancreas.

DNA. The common term for deoxyribonucleic acid, which contains the genetic information in the chromosomes.

DOMINANT. A gene that produces a visible trait even when it is paired with a different gene. The gene for brown eyes is dominant. A person with one gene for brown eyes and one gene for blue eyes will have brown eyes.

DROSOPHILIA. The scientific name of the common fruit fly. It is widely used in genetics because it reproduces quickly and is easy to raise in a lab.

ELEMENT. One of the substances composed of atoms, all of which have the same number of electrons and the same number of protons in the atomic nucleus. There are 103 elements, and some scientists report 104.

ENZYME. A protein produced by living cells that acts as a catalyst to speed up specific chemical reactions.

EPIGENESIS. The theory that material in the mother's womb, such as blood, develops into a baby in the presence of sperm.

FETUS. The unborn offspring after it has completed early embryonic development. In humans the offspring is called fetus from the third month of pregnancy to birth.

GENE. That section on a chromosome that contains the genetic information for a trait.

GENETICS. The science of heredity; the study of how traits are inherited.

GRAFTING. The process in which a twig of one plant is attached to the stem of another so that they grow together.

HOMUNCULUS. The name given to a perfectly formed but miniature human that was thought to exist in every sperm and that could mature only in a woman's womb.

HORMONES. Special proteins produced by glands and carried by the blood to regulate specific reactions in other cells, such as estrogen produced by the ovaries to regulate the reproductive cycle in animals.

HORTICULTURE. The science of plant cultivation.

HYBRID TRAIT. A trait carried by two different genes, a dominant and a recessive.

MICROBIOLOGIST. A scientist who studies organisms so small that they can be seen only with a microscope.

MICROTOME. A device that cuts thin sections of tissue for viewing under a microscope.

MITOSIS. The exact duplication of a cell's nucleus to form two identical nuclei, which usually takes place during cell division.

MOLECULE. The smallest part of a substance that will show the properties of that substance.

MUTATION. A sudden change in a trait that is inherited. It is caused by a change in a gene.

NITROGEN BASE. One of the three components of a nucleotide. Each nucleotide is made up of a five-carbon sugar, a phosphate group, and a nitrogen base. There are four nitrogen bases in DNA: adenine, thymine, cytosine, and guanine.

NUCLEIC ACIDS. Molecules, such as DNA an RNA, composed of long chains of nucleotides. They contain and transfer genetic information.

NUCLEOTIDES. The basic building blocks of nucleic acids. There are four in DNA: guanine, cytosine, adenine, and thymine. In RNA the thymine is replaced by uracil.

NUCLEUS. The structure in the cell that controls the activities of the cell and carries the hereditary material of the cell in the chromosomes.

OPAKE. An old spelling of the word opaque used by Robert Brown to describe the dark area he saw in cells and later identified as the nucleus.

OVARY. The sex organs of a female that produce both the eggs and the female sex hormones.

OZONE. A molecule of oxygen composed of three atoms of oxygen. Ozone forms a layer above our atmosphere that protects us from ultraviolet rays.

PARTHENOGENESIS. The growth and the development of an unfertilized egg. A drone bee, for example, is produced from an unfertilized egg.

PATHOLOGIST. A scientist who studies the origin, nature, and course of diseases.

PLASMID. A small circular piece of DNA carried by a bacterium. A plasmid can move in and out of a bacterial cell.

PROTEIN. Long chains of amino acids in specific order. Most of life's structures and functions are protein in nature.

PUREBRED TRAIT. A trait resulting from the combination of two like genes, either both dominant or both recessive.

RECESSIVE. A term given to a gene that is not expressed when the dominant gene is present, a trait that is expressed only when both genes are recessive. For example, you must have both recessive genes in order to have blue eyes.

RECOMBINANT DNA. A combination of two DNA molecules from different sources. Usually a piece of DNA from one species is spliced to a bacterial plasmid.

REGENERATION. The regrowth or replacement of a lost structure, such as the regrowth of the tail when a lizard loses it.

RIBOSOMES. The structures in a cell responsible for the production of proteins.

RNA. Ribonucleic acid. RNA is responsible for carrying genetic information from the DNA into the cytoplasm of the cell and placing the proper amino acids into positions to form their proteins. In some viruses, RNA carries the genetic message.

SEX-LINKED. A trait that is only on the X chromosome. Hemophilia and color blindness are sex-linked traits.

SPECIES. A group of organisms that interbreed and produce fertile offspring.

SPERM. The sex cell produced by the male animal containing one half the normal number of chromosomes for its species.

SPERMISTS. People who believed that Adam carried the sperm for all generations of people.

SPORTS. A common term used to describe an animal or plant with a visible mutation, such as short legs on sheep.

TISSUE. A group of cells that are specialized to perform a specific function.

TRANSDUCTION. The transfer of genetic material from one cell to another; for example, the way in which a virus can transfer genetic material from one bacterium to another.

UTERUS. The hollow muscular organ of the female in which the fetus develops; also called the womb.

VIRUS. A DNA or RNA molecule with a protein coat that can reproduce itself only in a living cell.

WOMB. A common term for the uterus, where the unborn offspring develops.

X-RAY DIFFRACTION. The process of analyzing the atomic structure of molecules with X-rays of crystals of that substance.

Bibliography

"All About That Baby." *Newsweek*, August 7, 1978, pp. 66–72.

Asimov, Isaac. *Asimov's Biographical Encyclopedia of Science and Technology*. New rev. ed. Garden City, N.Y.: Doubleday and Company, 1972.

———. *The Genetic Code*. New York: Signet Books, 1963.

———. *The Wellsprings of Life*. New York: First Signet Science Library, 1961.

Bottino, P. J. "Everything's Coming Up Violets: Cloning in the Classroom." *The Science Teacher*, Fall 1978, p. 54.

Bylinsky, Gene. "The Cloning Era Is Almost Here." *Fortune*, June 19, 1978, pp. 101–110.

"Cloning of a Man: Debate Begins." *Science News*, March 18, 1978, Vol. 113, No. 11, p. 164.

Dawkins, Richard. *The Selfish Gene*. New York: Oxford University Press, 1976.

Dougall, Donald K. "Plant Tissue Culture: The State of the Art." *Nurserymen's Digest*, February, 1976, pp. 72–81.

Etzioni, Amitai. *Genetic Fix*. New York: Macmillan Publishing Company, 1973.

"First Test Tube Baby." *Time*, July 31, 1978, pp. 58–70.

Gillie, Oliver. *The Living Cell*. New York: Funk and Wagnalls, 1971.

Goodfield, June. *Playing God: Genetic Engineering and the Manipulation of Life*. New York: Random House, 1977.

Grobstein, Clifford. "The Recombinant-DNA Debate." *Scientific American*, July 1977, Vol. 237, No. 1, pp. 22–23.

Halacy, D. S., Jr. *Genetic Revolution: Shaping Life for Tomorrow*. New York: Harper and Row, 1974.

Hartl, Daniel L. *Our Uncertain Heritage, Genetics and Human Diversity*. New York: J. B. Lippincott Company, 1977.

Hoagland, Mahlon B. *The Roots of Life: A Layman's Guide to Genes, Evolution, and the Ways of the Cells*. Boston: Houghton Mifflin Company, 1978.

Huxley, Aldous. *Brave New World*. New York: Harper and Row, 1946.

Hyde, Margaret. *The New Genetics*. New York: Franklin Watts, 1974.

Klein, Aaron E. *Threads of Life: Genetics From Aristotle to DNA*. New York: Natural History Press, 1970.

"Leakproof Lab . . . New Facility for DNA Work." *Time*, April 3, 1978, p. 70.

Lear, John. *Recombinant DNA, The Untold Story*. New York: Crown Publishers, 1978.

Lewin, Roger. "Profile of a Genetic Engineer." *New Scientist*, September 28, 1978, pp. 924–926.

McDonald, Phyllis Parshall. *Cloning and Genetic Engineering: Social and Legal Implications*. Kensington, Maryland: Kemtic Educational Corp., 1978.

Moore, Ruth. *The Coil of Life: The Story of the Great Discoveries in the Life Sciences*. New York: Alfred A. Knopf, 1967.

Payne, Alma Smith. *Discoverer of the Unseen World: A Biography of Antoine von Leeuwenhoek*. Cleveland: The World Publishing Company, 1966.

Rainis, Kenneth G. "Cloning, Is It the Step to Man?" *Ward's Bulletin*. Rochester, New York: Ward's Natural Science Establishment, Fall, 1978.

Rosenfeld, Albert. "The Case for Test Tube Babies." *Saturday Review*, October 28, 1978, pp. 10–14.

―――. *The Second Genesis: The Coming Control of Life*. Englewood Cliffs, N.J.: Prentice Hall, 1968.

Sayre, Anne. *Rosalind Franklin and DNA*. New York: W. W. Norton and Company, 1975.

Silverstein, Alvin and Virginia. *The Code of Life*. New York: Atheneum, 1972.

"Test Tube Baby." *Time*, July 24, 1978, p. 47.

Thomas, Lewis. *The Lives of A Cell*. New York: The Viking Press, 1974.

Tufty, Barbara. *Cells, Units of Life*. New York: G. P. Putnam's Sons, 1973.

Watson, James D. *The Double Helix*. New York: Atheneum, 1968.

Index

Numbers in boldface refer to illustrations.